Contents

Ancient Egypt

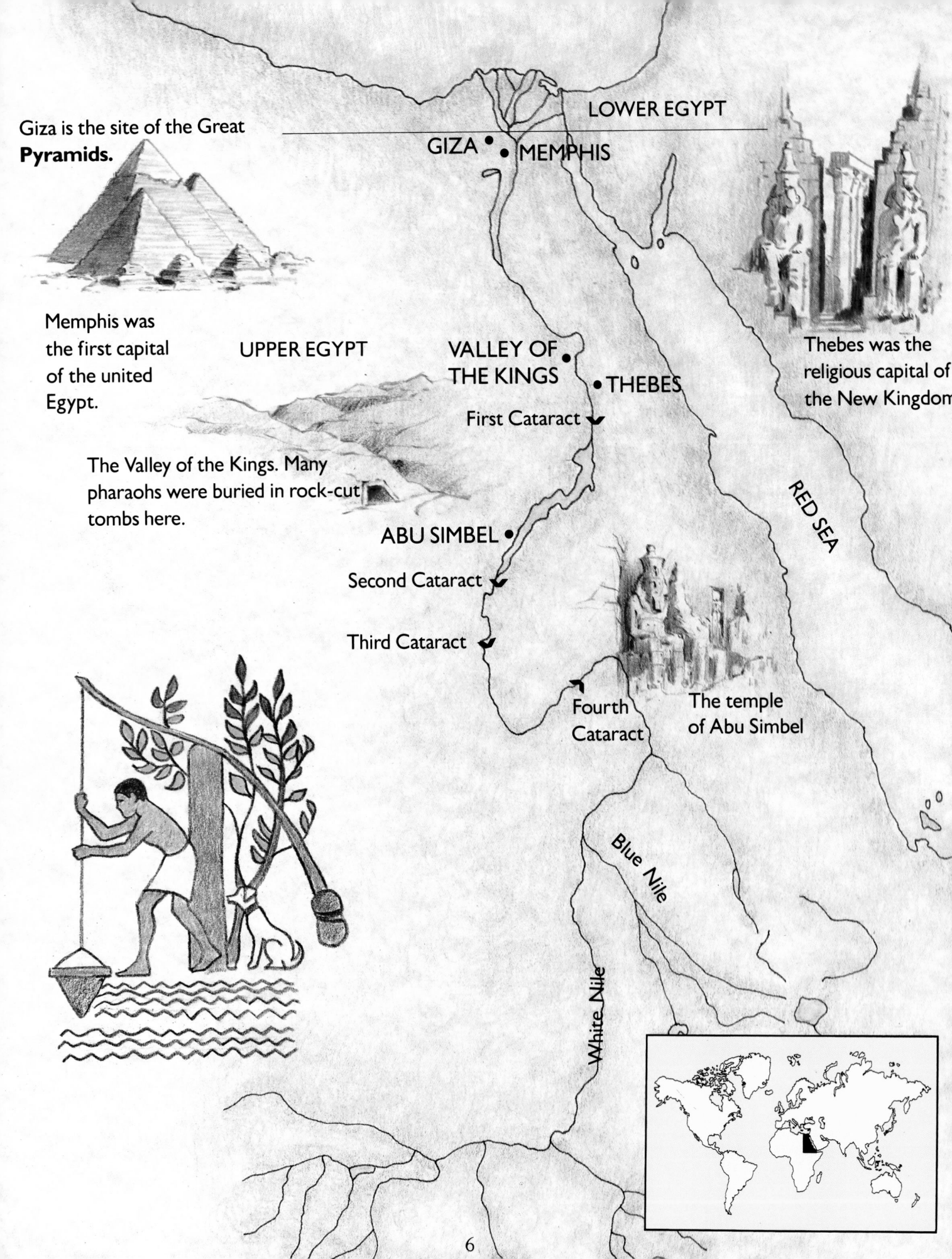

LOWER EGYPT

GIZA • • MEMPHIS

Giza is the site of the Great **Pyramids.**

Memphis was the first capital of the united Egypt.

UPPER EGYPT

VALLEY OF THE KINGS •
• THEBES
First Cataract

Thebes was the religious capital of the New Kingdom

The Valley of the Kings. Many pharaohs were buried in rock-cut tombs here.

ABU SIMBEL •

Second Cataract

RED SEA

Third Cataract

Fourth Cataract

The temple of Abu Simbel

Blue Nile

White Nile

The Egyptian World

The great **civilisation** of ancient Egypt began over 5,000 years ago, when Menes, the ruler of Upper Egypt, overcame Lower Egypt and united the two kingdoms. The Egyptians never forgot that Egypt had once been two lands, and the **pharaoh** was known as *king of Upper and Lower Egypt*.

For the next 3,000 years Egypt remained strong and powerful and gradually expanded to take over new lands. The Egyptians were a sophisticated people who developed architecture and new efficient methods of government and made important discoveries in medicine and astronomy.

The Gift of the Nile

Egypt is a long, thin country running along the length of the Nile, an oasis surrounded by desert. A Greek arriving in Egypt for the first time called the country *the gift of the Nile*, because it was the Nile which provided most of Egypt's wealth. The rest of Egypt is barren and rocky with little water.

This desert, which the ancient Egyptians called *the Red Land*, cannot support much life, although precious stones and metals are found there. Once a year the **Akhet** or **Inundation** came, flooding the river valley from July to September and leaving behind rich, fertile black mud, *the Black Land*. The amount of water brought by the floods was critical: too little meant that the crops would fail and there would be famine, too much and houses, livestock and people would be swept away by the river. For this reason, the water level was

constantly checked with a measure known as a **nilometer**, and the changing seasons were carefully monitored to try to prevent famine. In order to read the seasons the Egyptians studied the cycle of the Sun, the Moon and the stars, which led them to divide the year up into 365 days, made up of 12 months each with 30 days and 5 extra days.

◀ The Egyptians also depended on the Nile for transport. They did not usually use carts with wheels, as these were useless in the desert sands or in the mud. Heavy loads were dragged to and from river barges on rollers or sledges.

▼ The green and fertile land around the Nile stands out against the barren desert that surrounds it.

The Pharaoh

The pharaoh of Egypt was an absolute ruler, answerable to no-one. Whatever he decided was the law. In fact one way to say *justice* was "what the pharaoh loves" and to say *wrong-doing* was "what the pharaoh hates".

The pharaoh was considered to be a god. He married his own sister or half-sister so that his children would have the blood of the gods. He often had many other wives too. His subjects treated him with all the reverence they gave to their other gods, kneeling before him with their foreheads touching the ground. As a sign of respect they never referred to him by his own name, but used official names instead. One of these was *great house* or *per-ao*, which is where our word pharaoh comes from.

A complex administrative system was set up to deal with the governing of the five million people in the empire. The pharaoh's chief adviser or **vizier** was the second most powerful man in the kingdom, standing in for the pharaoh and deciding what matters were important enough for the pharaoh's ears. Under the vizier's rule were numerous local governors called **nomarchs** who were each in charge of a region or nome. They ensured that everyone paid their taxes, which were in the form of goods or services as the Egyptians did not use money.

▼ With all the different religious and administrative obligations upon him, the pharaoh had very little time to himself.

Famous Pharaohs

In the 3,000 years when Egypt was powerful there were over 300 pharaohs. Some were great warriors and some helped to establish the strong government of Egypt, but we know very little about most of them apart from their names.

Tutankhamen

Tutankhamen was just a boy when he became pharaoh. His reign lasted for only ten years but he restored order to the country after the previous pharaoh, Akenaten, had caused chaos by trying to introduce a new religion. Tutankhamen started building a number of huge temples to honour the god Amun-Re.

Tuthmosis III

Tuthmosis, the greatest of the warrior pharaohs, conquered Palestine and Syria and never lost a battle.

Cleopatra VII

Cleopatra was one of the few women to become pharaoh in her own right. She tried to form a political alliance with the Roman empire, first through **Julius Caesar** and then by marrying **Mark Antony**. After a huge military defeat she killed herself.

Gods and Temples

Religion was a very important part of Egyptian life. There were gods to deal with every imaginable event or problem. These gods often took on the shape or part of the shape of a particular animal. For example Bast, the goddess of joy and love, was usually shown as a cat and Anubis, the god who protected the tombs of the dead, was shown either as a jackal or a man with a jackal's head.

Each god had a temple where people could come to worship and ask favours. A statue of the god stood in a room at the back of the temple. It was only brought out on feast days and even then the statue itself was kept hidden inside a shrine. Ordinary people could only go as far as the entrance hall of the temple, where they would meet the god's servant, the priest. The priest would take messages and offerings from the people and interpret the god's answers. Often the animals associated with the god were kept in the temple.

The temple was considered to be the home of the god. Each day meals were laid before his statue for the god to eat if he chose. Later the food was removed and eaten by the priests.

▼ The temple of Amun at Karnak was extended by pharaoh after pharaoh until it was the size of six huge cathedrals.

Important Gods

RE was the sun god. He took on different shapes at different times of the day.

AMUN was the god of the air and of Thebes. His name means *hidden*. When Thebes became the capital of Egypt, he merged with Re to become the chief god, Amun-Re.

OSIRIS was the god of the dead, who judged all men when they died.

ISIS was the sister-wife of Osiris and the goddess and protector of women.

AMUN   OSIRIS   ISIS

▶ This wall-painting shows Hathor, goddess of music and love, in the form of a cow.

▲ The Jackal was sacred to Anubis, god of the dead.

The Afterlife

The Egyptians believed firmly that with proper preparation a person could live again after death. This preparation involved preserving the body of the dead person and providing it with all the food, furniture, tools and riches which it was thought would be needed in the afterlife. Even the poorest people were buried with scraps of food.

Journey to the Afterlife

The dead person had to make a long and hazardous journey before he could enjoy the pleasures of the afterlife. He had to pass a giant serpent and a crocodile, avoid being caught in fishing nets and a fiery furnace, and escape from people trying to drown him and chop his head off.

When the dead man reached the underworld, the god Anubis measured his heart against the Feather of Truth. If they balanced, he would be greeted by Osiris, but if not, he would be devoured by a monster which was part-crocodile, part-lion and part-hippopotamus.

▼ In this painting Anubis weighs the heart of the dead person, while Osiris waits to greet him. Thoth, god of wisdom, records what is happening. Which do you think is the dead person? Can you find the eleven judges?

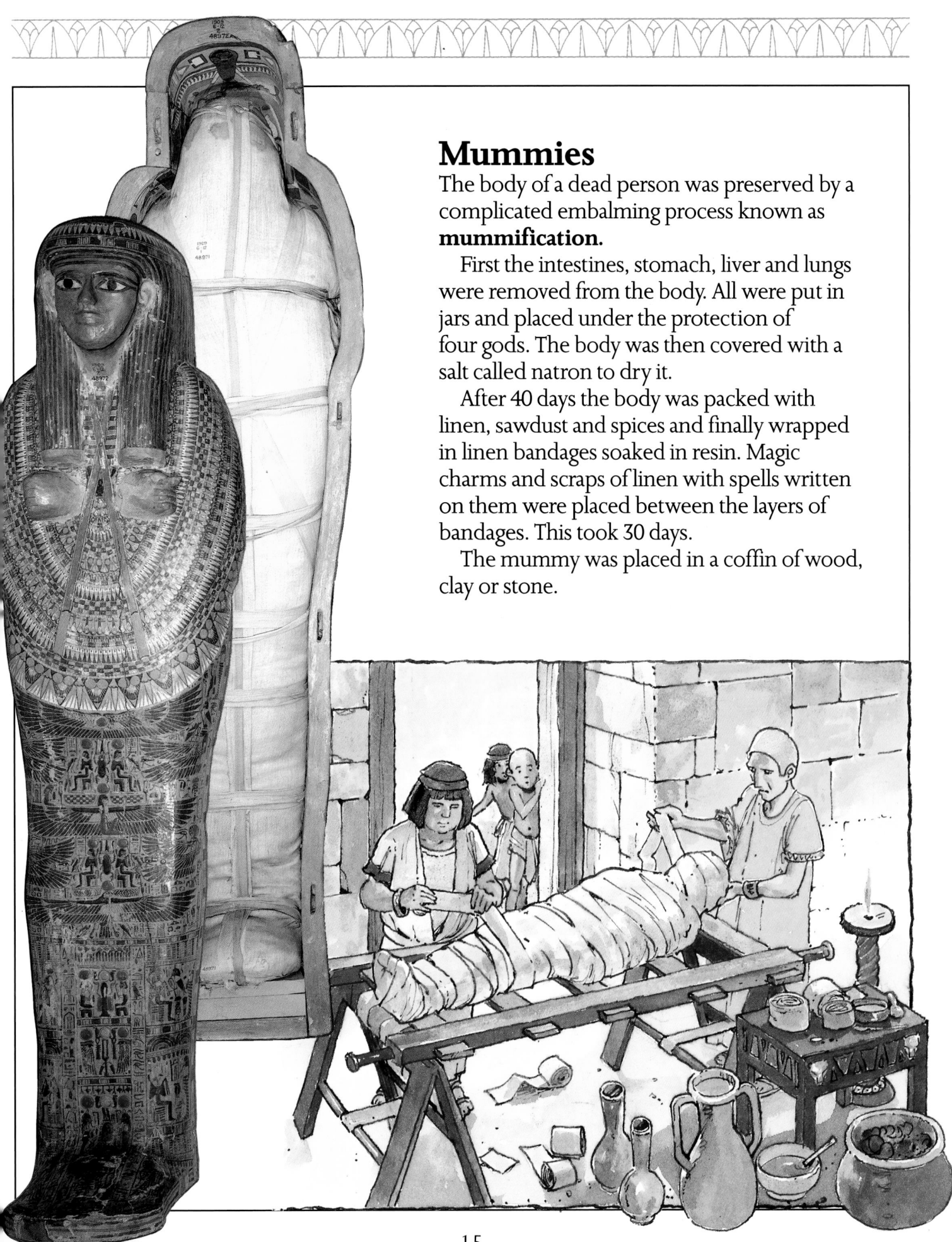

Mummies

The body of a dead person was preserved by a complicated embalming process known as **mummification.**

First the intestines, stomach, liver and lungs were removed from the body. All were put in jars and placed under the protection of four gods. The body was then covered with a salt called natron to dry it.

After 40 days the body was packed with linen, sawdust and spices and finally wrapped in linen bandages soaked in resin. Magic charms and scraps of linen with spells written on them were placed between the layers of bandages. This took 30 days.

The mummy was placed in a coffin of wood, clay or stone.

The Pyramids

The tombs of the pharaohs were huge and elaborate and took many years to build. The pyramids were the tombs of some of the early pharaohs. Such were the riches inside that tomb-robbing became very common, and later pharaohs had maze-like tombs hidden underground. Most of these were eventually discovered by tomb robbers.

▼ Each of the blocks of stone used to build the pyramid had to be hauled into place by hand. Ramps of packed earth were built first to move the stone up to the level where it was needed.

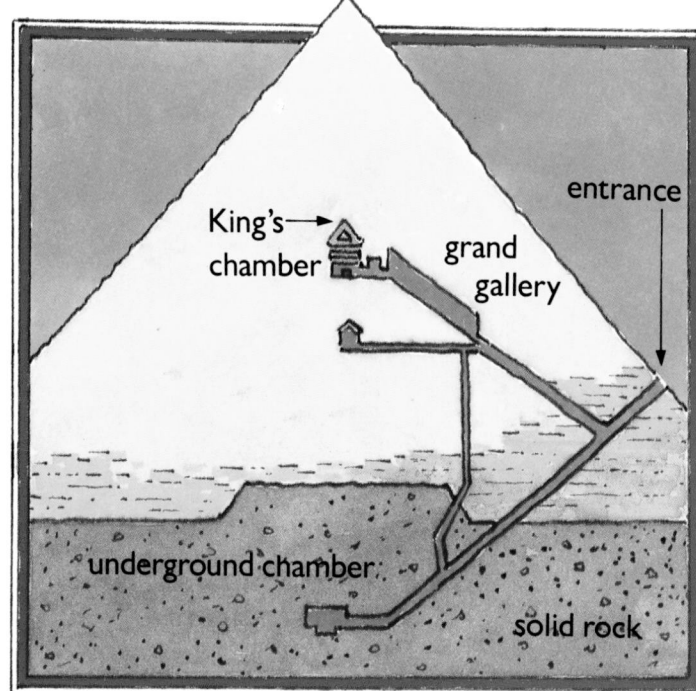

▲ Inside the Great Pyramid.

▼ The Great Pyramid at Giza was originally 147m tall. It contained over two million blocks of stone, each weighing about 2.5 tonnes, although some of them weighed up to 14 tonnes. It was covered in highly polished limestone which gleamed in the Sun. It took 50,000 people 20 years to build.

▲ Large blocks of stone could be lifted using wooden wedges.

Writing and Education

Early Egyptians wrote using picture letters called **hieroglyphs**. There were over 700 of these letters, some of which stood for whole words. The word signs were simple pictures illustrating an object or action. For example, a series of wavy lines were drawn to mean water. Other signs stood for one or two letters. There were no vowels in the alphabet, but the Egyptians managed quite well without them. Try writing in English with no vowels – you should still find it quite easy to read.

Gradually hieroglyphs became less detailed to make them quicker and easier to write. This form of writing was used by scribes for everyday documents, such as records of taxes. Hieroglyphs were still used for writing on tombs and monuments.

The Egyptians did not use paper but wrote on **papyrus**, made from reed stems which had been flattened, dried and stuck together to make pages. A thin, sharpened reed dipped in ink was used to write with.

▲ Many paintings in tombs include writing that explains what is happening in the picture.

Learning

Most people could not read or write. Children were usually taught a trade or craft by their parents. There were some schools where boys training to be scribes were taught writing, mathematics and astronomy. They learnt to read and write by copying and chanting wisdom texts which gave advice on morals and behaviour. These schools cannot have been very pleasant places to be, as the children were regularly beaten. One scribe wrote "the ears of a boy are in his back. He listens only when he is beaten".

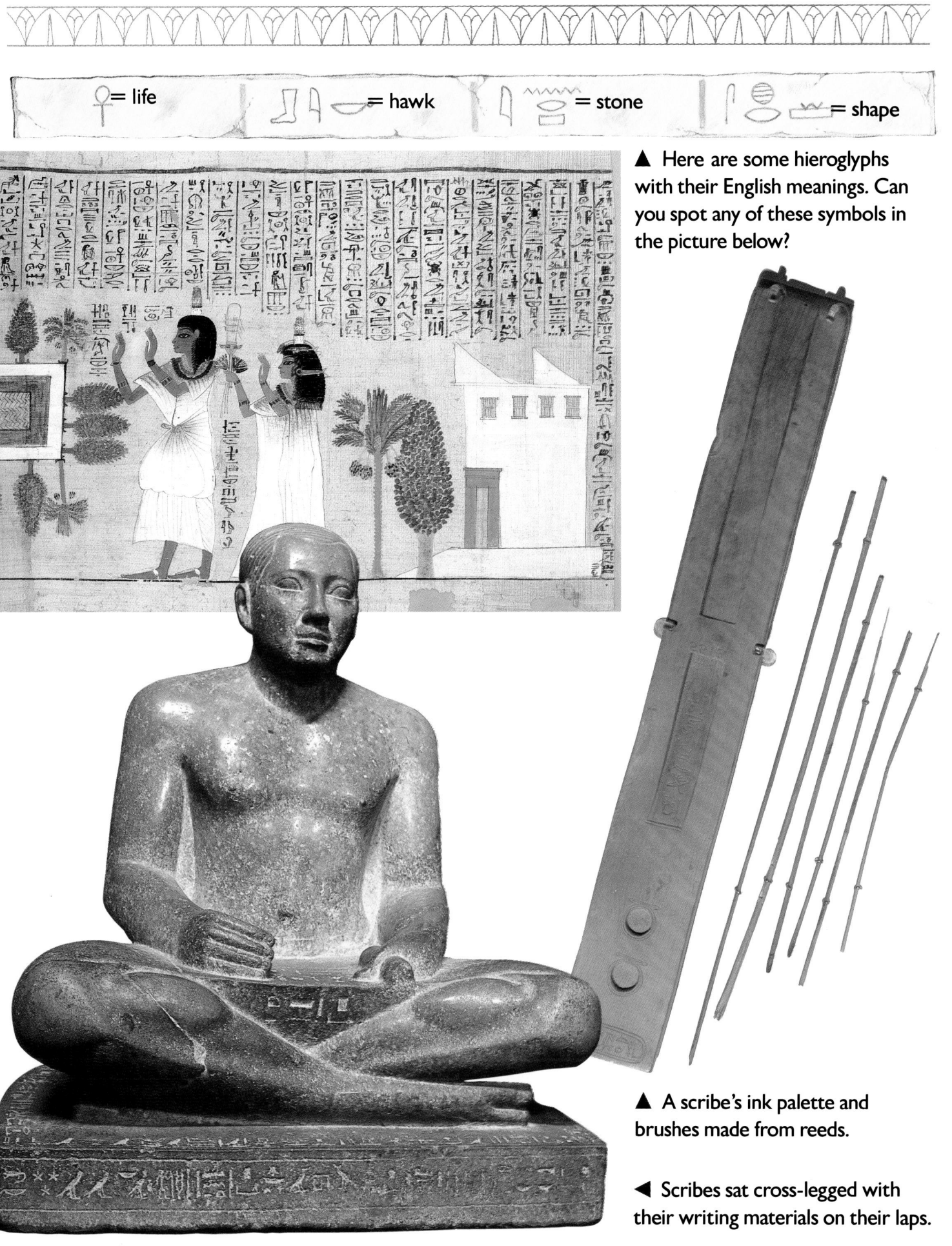

= life

= hawk

= stone

= shape

▲ Here are some hieroglyphs with their English meanings. Can you spot any of these symbols in the picture below?

▲ A scribe's ink palette and brushes made from reeds.

◀ Scribes sat cross-legged with their writing materials on their laps.

At Home

Egyptian houses were clustered together on the higher ground at the edge of the river's flood area. They were built of sun-baked brick made from mud and straw. In Egypt's hot, dry climate these bricks lasted a long time. Only buildings which were expected to last for eternity, like temples and tombs, were built of stone.

Houses were very plain, square buildings. They were often surrounded by a wall and had steps outside leading to a flat roof. Inside, the house was dark because of the tiny windows.

The front room of an ordinary house was used by the man of the family to conduct his trade. Sometimes people even kept livestock in this room. There was little furniture in the houses of ordinary people, just a chest for clothes, and storage jars for food.

The second room was usually large with windows high up in the walls. This was used for receiving guests and eating meals. The kitchen, bathroom and bedrooms were at the back of the house.

Sometimes cooking was done on the flat roofs of the houses to avoid the risk of fire.

The houses of the rich looked similar to ordinary houses from the outside, although they were larger. Inside they were decorated with wall paintings and panelling, where they were protected from the cutting desert winds.

Furniture Facts

● The Egyptians used little furniture. Poor people usually had none, and even the rich often sat on the floor.

● Much of the furniture was portable, like this folding wooden stool (right), which would have had a leather seat.

● Beds, like most furniture, were made from wood and reeds. Wooden head-rests were used instead of pillows.

Work and Play

Work

Most Egyptians were farmers but some had other jobs. As well as priests, scribes and government officials, there were all sorts of craftsmen. Building projects like the pyramids required hundreds of skilled men: draughtsmen to design the structure, masons to carve the stone, painters to decorate the walls, sculptors to carve the statues and other craftsmen to make all the furniture, jewellery, tools and utensils which were to be put inside.

As the Egyptians did not use money, the craftsmen were paid with food, drink, clothes and lodging. Sometimes the men working on royal tombs went on strike if their payment did not turn up.

▶ Egyptian craftsmen used tools made from wood, bronze and other metals.

22

Play

Egyptians worked very hard – sometimes for eight days in a row, followed by two days off. They spent much of their spare time very actively: hunting, dancing and playing athletic games like wrestling, ball games and acrobatics. Rich people held sumptuous dinner parties, where guests were entertained by acrobats and musicians.

Board games were popular and **senet** was the favourite. It was played on a board divided into three rows of ten squares. Each player had seven pieces and the aim was to get all your pieces to the end of the board, whilst preventing your opponent from doing the same.

Children played with wooden balls and tops as well as dolls and carved wooden animals.

▲ Some Egyptian toys had moving parts. This cat's jaw is operated with a string, and the wooden horse moves along on its wheels.

► This senet board has a little drawer to keep the pieces in when they are not being used.

▼ Do you know what games these children are playing?

23

Food

The fertile soil around the Nile helped produce a wide variety of crops for the Egyptian people. There was a plentiful supply of wheat and barley for bread and beer. Vegetables such as onions, leeks, lettuce and all kinds of beans were eaten in great quantities. They were often served with an oil and vinegar dressing, rather like modern salad dressing. There was less fruit because it was harder to grow in the extremes of the Egyptian climate. However, the Egyptians did manage to grow figs, dates and pomegranates, and grapes to make wine.

People did not eat a great deal of meat. Cattle were more often kept as beasts of burden and for milk than for meat. Feasts for the rich included a wide variety of meats though, including such strange delicacies as antelope and hyena. Fish was eaten mostly by the poor.

The Egyptians ate from low tables seated on the floor. They used their fingers to eat with. The pharaoh had a servant to wash his hands between each course.

Egyptian Bread

Try making your own Egyptian bread. You can add chopped dates to the dough if you like.

You will need:
400 g wholemeal flour
225 ml water
½ tsp salt

- Add the water to the flour and salt quite slowly, mixing thoroughly.
- Knead the dough.
- Shape into small rounds or triangles.
- Cover with a cloth and leave overnight.
- Bake for 30 minutes at 180°C.

Mix up the ingredients.

Knead the dough.

Cover the dough overnight before baking.

Farming Facts

● There were three seasons in the farming year: the Inundation (June – October), the Emergence (November – January) when the floodwaters subsided, and the Drought (February – June).

● Each farmer's land was marked by heavy stones which could not be moved by the floods.

● A complex irrigation system allowed flood water to be stored in huge reservoirs so that it could be used when needed.

● During the Inundation, when little farmwork could be done, many people worked on the pharaoh's building projects as a way of paying their taxes.

▲ Egyptian farmers used wooden ploughs drawn by oxen.

Clothes

The clothes worn by most Egyptian people were made from linen. Flax, which linen is made from, grows well in the Egyptian climate, and the fabric is cool and comfortable. Most people wore undyed linen, decorated by pleating. Only the rich could afford brightly coloured cloth.

Men wore a length of linen wrapped around their waists like a kilt or a simple tunic. Labourers usually wore linen loincloths or nothing at all. Men were usually clean-shaven or had small, pointed beards.

Women wore ankle-length dresses, often with one or both shoulders bare.

Most children wore no clothes and had their heads shaved, except for a long plait on the right side of their head which was called "the lock of youth". In cold weather everyone except the priests wore cloaks of wool or animal skins. Sandals were made from reeds or leather, with a strap over the instep and between the first and second toes.

▲ Egyptian mirrors were made of bronze, and combs of ivory or wood.

Egyptian Cosmetics

● Personal appearance was very important to the Egyptians. They used perfumed oils to keep their skin healthy in the harsh desert winds.

● Rich Egyptian men and women wore wigs made from a mixture of real hair and vegetable fibres. The strands were fixed to a netting base with wax.

● Men and women wore eye make-up to protect their eyes from sand and dust.

● At dinner parties guests and servants wore cones of perfumed oil on their heads. The perfume gradually melted and ran down their hair and clothes.

Nut's Children

The ancient Egyptians told many stories about their gods and about the world around them. Often these stories would try to explain something that the people did not really understand. Nut's Children tries to explain why the Moon waxes and wanes.

In long ago times, Re, the chief of all the gods, still reigned on Earth as a living pharaoh. He lived in a huge palace on the banks of the Nile, and all the people of Egypt came to bow down before him. All his courtiers did exactly what he asked, and he spent his time hunting, playing games and feasting. It was a wonderful life!

However, one day a courtier came to him and told him about a conversation he had overheard. Thoth, god of wisdom and magic, had told the goddess Nut that one day her son would be Pharaoh of Egypt.

Re was furious. How could anyone but he possibly be Pharaoh? No-one else was worthy of the task, and besides, he had no intention of

ever giving up the throne. He raged about in his chambers, shouting at the top of his voice.

"How dare they suggest such a thing! Why, they are probably plotting to get rid of me at this very moment. But no child of Nut will de-throne me!"

He thought and thought about a way to protect his throne. Eventually, summoning all the magic powers he possessed, he spoke these words: "I lay this curse upon her: no child of Nut will be born on any day or any night of any year."

News travelled quickly amongst the gods, so Nut soon heard of Re's curse. She was quite heart-broken. She badly wanted a child, but she knew that Re's magic was very strong. How could she break the curse? The only person who might be able to help her was Thoth, wisest of all gods, so she set off to see him at once.

Thoth loved Nut dearly and, when he saw her tears, he decided at once to do all he could to help her.

"I cannot lift Re's curse," he said, "but I may be able to get round it. Just wait here."

Thoth knew that Khonsu, the Moon god, was a great gambler, so he went to visit him and challenged him to a game of senet.

Khonsu did not stop to think for a moment. He could not resist the challenge.

"O, Thoth," he said. "You may be the wisest of all the gods, but I am the greatest senet player there has ever been. I have never lost a game. I will certainly play you and I will win every game easily!"

The two sat down to play. From the very start, Thoth won every game. All seven of his pieces seemed to reach the far end of the board before Khonsu's pieces had even moved.

"You have just been lucky up till now, Thoth," said Khonsu. "I wager an hour of my light that I will win the next game."

But still he lost! Thoth kept on winning and Khonsu kept on wagering his own light until Thoth had won enough of Khonsu's light to make up five whole days. Then Thoth stood up, thanked Khonsu for the game and left, taking Khonsu's light with him.

"What a coward," muttered Khonsu to himself. "My luck was just starting to change. I would certainly have won the next game!"

Thoth fitted the five extra days in between the end of that year and the beginning of the next. Until that time the year had been made up of twelve months, each with 30 days, making a total of 360 days in the year. That number remained the same, but the five extra days set the calendar right.

Nut was overjoyed when Thoth told her what he had done. Because the five extra days

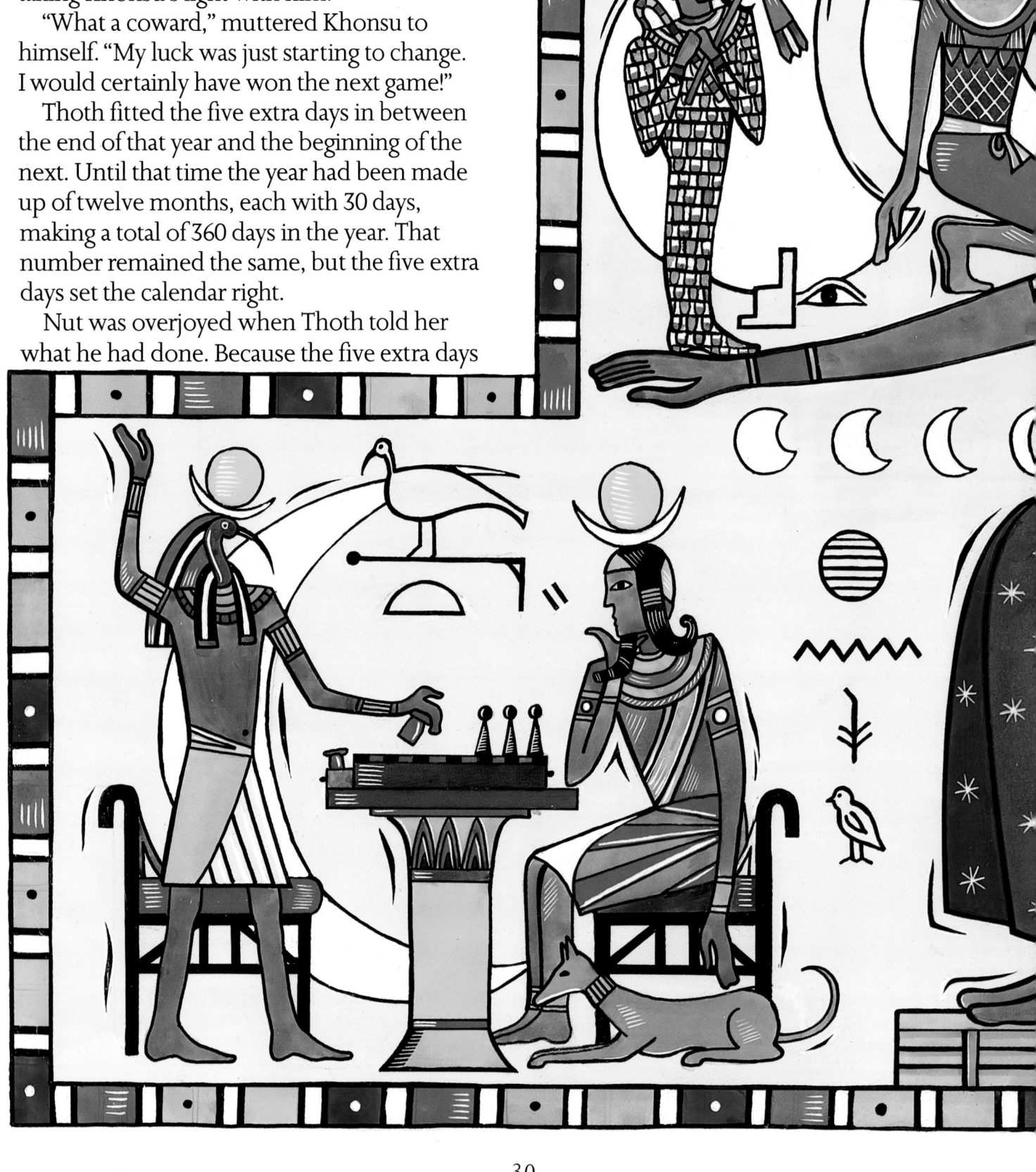

were not days in any year, Nut's children could be born on these days without breaking Re's curse. On the first day Nut gave birth to Osiris, who was to be Pharaoh after Re; on the second day to Harmachis, who is immortalised as the Sphinx; on the third day Set, who later killed Osiris and became Pharaoh for a while; on the fourth day Isis, who was to be the wife of Osiris, and on the fifth day Nephthys, who was to be Set's wife.

As for Khonsu the Moon god, he was so weakened after the game with Thoth that he lost much of his strength for ever. He could no longer shine brightly all the time. Even today the Moon only shines brightly on a few days of the month and has to spend the rest of the time gathering its strength together.

How We Know

Have you ever wondered how we know so much about the lives of the ancient Egyptians, although they lived thousands of years ago?

Evidence from the Ground

Archaeologists have found many objects which were thrown away by ancient Egyptians and which have been preserved by the hot, dry climate of Egypt. They have also built up a very clear picture of everyday life from the objects found in tombs and the paintings on the walls.

▲ Tomb-paintings like this one give a detailed picture of life in ancient Egypt.

Evidence around Us

Many people in Egypt today have a lifestyle similar to that of the ancient Egyptians of thousands of years ago. Farmers on the banks of the Nile still live in houses built of sun-baked brick, following the same pattern as the ancient houses, and certain farming methods are the same. A huge dam built on the Nile now controls the flooding of the river and makes people's lives much easier.

Evidence from Books

The Egyptians were great writers. Scribes recorded everything that happened in minute detail, and many of these records survive today. It is thanks to them that we know more about the Egyptians than we do about many peoples who have lived since them.

▲ It was not until 1822, some time after the **Rosetta Stone** had been discovered, that Egyptian texts could be read. The same text was written on it in hieroglyphs, an Egyptian script called **demotic** and Greek. A Frenchman called Campolian used this and other monuments to find the key to hieroglyphs.

Ancient Greece

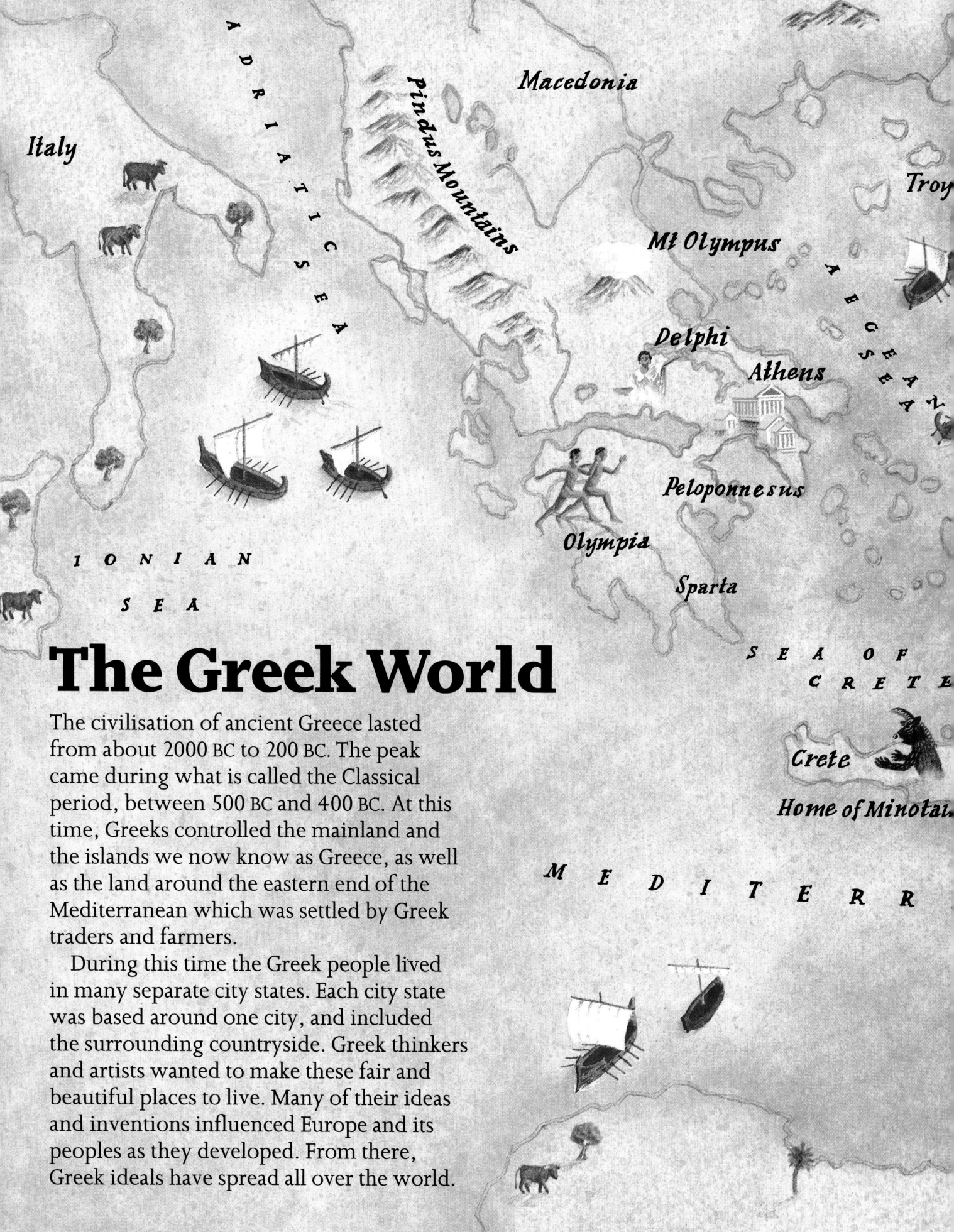

Italy

A D R I A T I C   S E A

Pindus Mountains

Macedonia

Troy

Mt Olympus

A E G E A N

Delphi

Athens

Peloponnesus

Olympia

Sparta

I O N I A N

S E A

S E A   O F
C R E T E

Crete

Home of Minotaur

M E D I T E R R A

The Greek World

The civilisation of ancient Greece lasted
from about 2000 BC to 200 BC. The peak
came during what is called the Classical
period, between 500 BC and 400 BC. At this
time, Greeks controlled the mainland and
the islands we now know as Greece, as well
as the land around the eastern end of the
Mediterranean which was settled by Greek
traders and farmers.

During this time the Greek people lived
in many separate city states. Each city state
was based around one city, and included
the surrounding countryside. Greek thinkers
and artists wanted to make these fair and
beautiful places to live. Many of their ideas
and inventions influenced Europe and its
peoples as they developed. From there,
Greek ideals have spread all over the world.

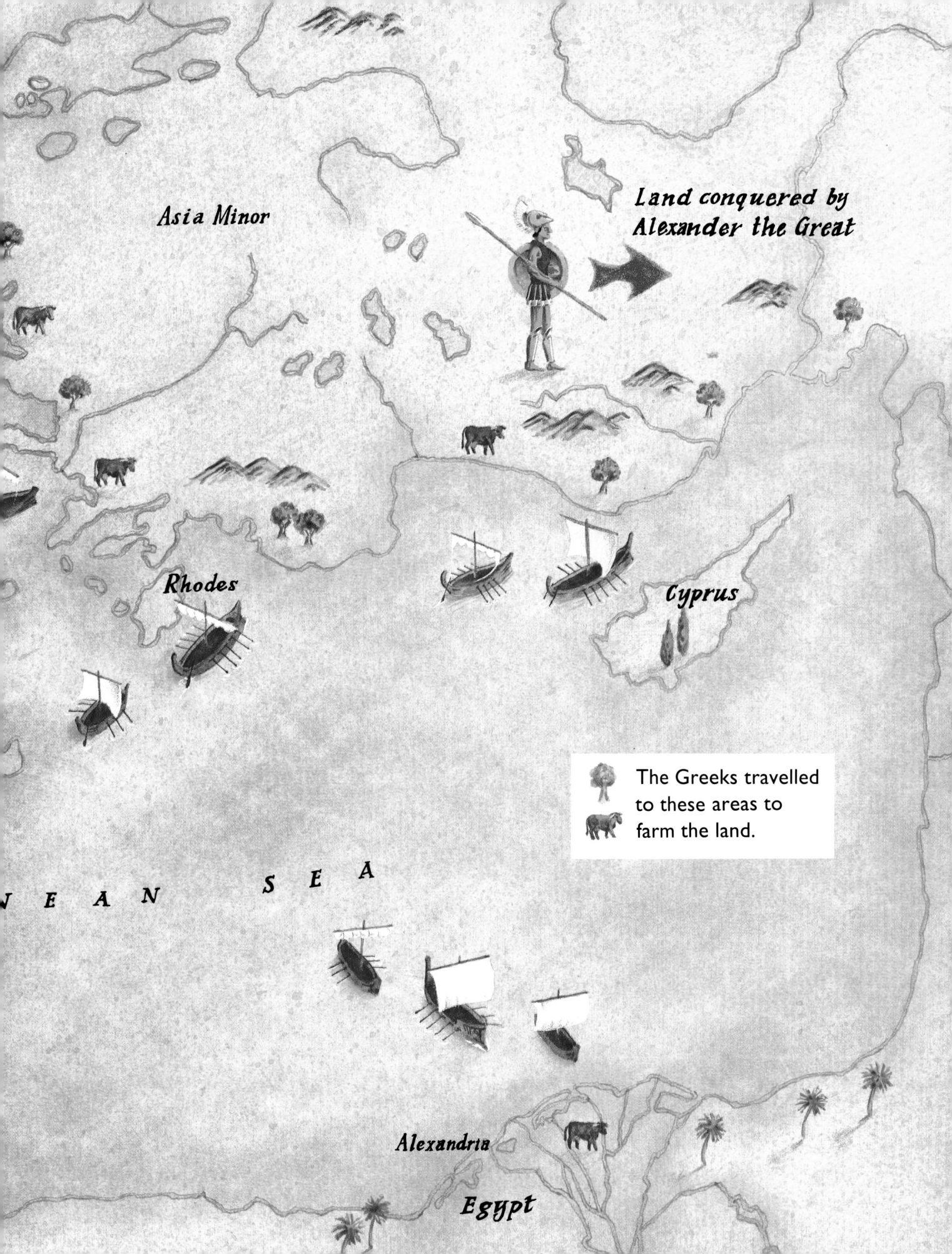

Asia Minor

Land conquered by
Alexander the Great

Rhodes

Cyprus

The Greeks travelled
to these areas to
farm the land.

N E A N   S E A

Alexandria

Egypt

Greek Lands

Mainland Greece and the islands which surround it are hot and dry with many high mountains and steep-sided valleys. Its hills and valleys were once heavily wooded but by the Classical period many of the forests had been cut down. The Greek mainland is surrounded almost entirely by water.

Farmland was scarce because of the rugged countryside, and was mainly near the coast and in sheltered valleys, where the most important crops were wheat, barley, grapes and olives. However, the Greeks were skilled sailors and keen traders which meant that they could import food.

Small village communities were very isolated from one another, because of the high mountains and steep valleys. There were very few roads, and most journeys had to be made on foot.

▲ As travel overland was so difficult, the Greeks travelled whenever possible by sea. Stormy seas and rugged coasts meant that this could be very dangerous. Sailors had no compasses and had to navigate by the stars.

▶ Olive trees growing on a dry, rocky hillside.

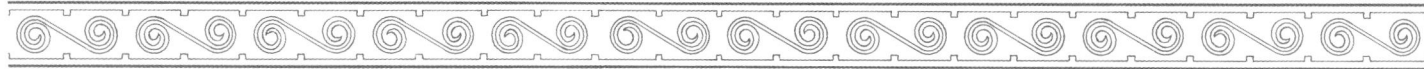

City States

Greece was not one united country as it is today. Instead it was made up of separate city states. A city state or **polis** was based around one city, and included all the surrounding farms, villages and houses.

Athens was the city of education and learning. Athenian philosophers, politicians and artists were famous throughout Greece. About 300,000 people lived in the city itself and the surrounding countryside.

Sparta was Athens' greatest rival. Sparta was famed for the strength of her army. There were many wars between the two cities, which were trying to gain control of the whole of Greece.

▼ This is the ancient city of Athens. The Acropolis, which means high city, was easy to defend in times of war. The main temple of the city, the Parthenon, was built on this hill.

The Peloponnesian War

The rivalry between Athens and Sparta eventually led to the Peloponnesian War (431 to 404 BC). Sparta attacked Athens first, fearful of the city's growing power. After many triumphs and setbacks, Sparta won the war, but both states were weakened after 27 years of fighting.

▶ Their only defence was their bronze shields.

▲ This vase painting shows Greek soldiers, armed with shields, spears and swords.

▲ Greek soldiers used a variety of weapons: spears, javelins, daggers, arrows, slingshot.

Citizens and Slaves

In Greek cities, there were groups of people with different rights and different roles to play in society. **Citizens** were the most important and had the most rights. They could own property and take part in politics and the law.

In Athens and some other cities, most male adults were citizens. Women, **slaves** and foreigners were not. In Sparta, far fewer were citizens. Only men from the richest families had citizen's rights, which meant only one in ten adult men.

Slaves were usually captured prisoners of war. They were owned by the people they worked for, and were bought and sold like property. Some lived quite comfortably with the families they worked for. Others lived in miserable conditions or toiled in mines until they died. Most slaves were paid for much of the work they did. If they saved enough money, they could buy their freedom.

▲ Each Greek city minted its own coins, stamped with the city symbol, such as the owl of Athens.

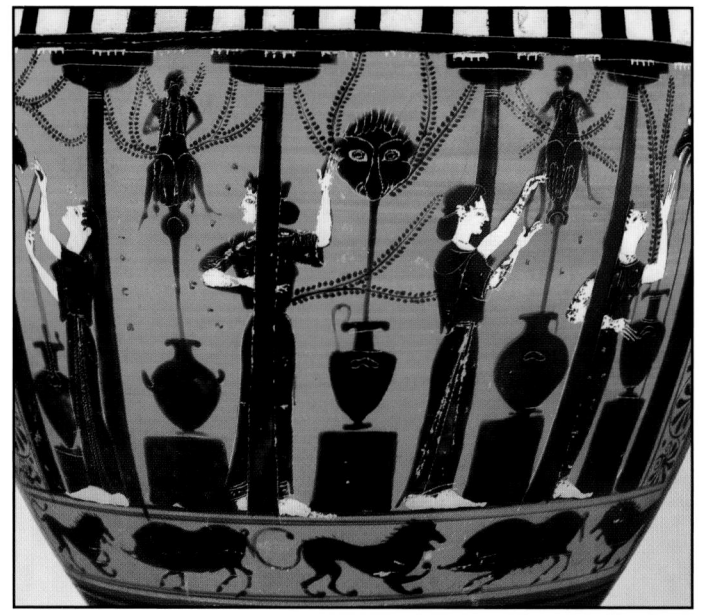

▲ This vase painting shows women slaves drawing water from a fountain.

Government

Many of the city states of Ancient Greece were **democracies**. In a democracy, the decisions about government were taken by councils of ordinary citizens. Only adult men were entitled to be citizens. Some city states, however, were ruled by rich and powerful landowners, supported by armies.

In Athens, all citizens voted to decide how the city was run, what taxes to pay, whether to go to war and so on. Poor workers were even paid a full day's wages to attend the government assemblies. There were no separate politicians or lawyers in Athens. All citizens took part in politics and legal affairs.

▲ Jurymen used discs such as these to vote in courts of law. Hollow discs indicated 'guilty', solid 'not guilty'.

▲ Citizens could vote to banish politicians by writing their names on these pottery fragments, called **ostraka**.

Philosophers and Scientists

The ancient Greeks were very curious about themselves and the world around them and made many important advances in science, learning and art. Great thinkers were known as **philosophers** no matter what subject they studied. The word philosophy comes from the Greek words for 'love of wisdom'. Philosophers tried to find out how the universe worked, why people were good or evil, and how people should live their lives.

Many Greek discoveries provide the foundations of our knowledge and beliefs.

Greeks studied the stars and discovered that the Earth floated freely in space, turning on its own axis. They also correctly predicted eclipses of the sun. Sometimes they were wrong. Ptolemy, a Greek scholar, thought the Earth was the centre of the Universe.

Most new ideas were never used for solving practical problems. Metal-working techniques, for example, were still primitive and never developed enough to make tools which could take advantage of the advances made in science.

Famous Philosophers

● **Hippocrates** (about 460 – 377 BC)
Hippocrates founded a medical school, where he practised scientific medicine instead of magic or religion. He taught the value of knowing how the body worked.

● **Aristotle** (384 – 322 BC)
Aristotle examined living things in nature. He also wrote on many subjects, including politics, and invented a method of thinking called logic.

● **Socrates** (about 469 – 399 BC)
Socrates, one of the first great philosophers of Classical Greece, taught the value of questioning common beliefs in order to find new ideas and explore new truths.

▲ Bust of Socrates.

● **Plato** (about 427 – 347 BC)
Plato founded a school for philosophers called The Academy where he taught Aristotle. His famous books are *The Republic* and *Dialogues*.

◄ The Greek philosopher Eratosthenes calculated the circumference of the Earth by measuring the angle of the sun at Alexandria in northern Egypt, and measuring the distance from there to Syene in southern Egypt, where the sun was overhead at noon. His figure for the circumference was correct to within 320 km

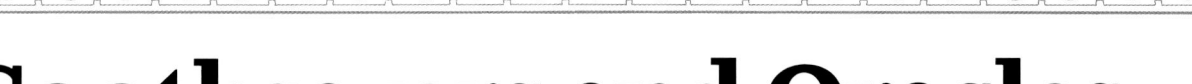

Soothsayers and Oracles

The Greeks had many gods and goddesses who usually represented a particular aspect of life, such as love or war. Most of them were believed to live on **Mount Olympus**. The Greeks told stories about their gods, in which they fought and loved, and were angry or jealous just like men and women.

Many of the gods had temples where priests or priestesses performed rituals in their honour. Gods were often honoured by **sacrifices**. Usually these were just gifts of food and wine but, on big feast days or festivals, many animals were sacrificed.

The Greeks looked to the gods for anwers to all their problems. For simple questions, such as "Should I marry this man?" they would go to a **soothsayer**. He or she would study the weather or the insides of a sacrificed animal to find the gods' answer.

For more complicated questions, like "how should we defeat our enemies?" a visit to an **oracle** was necessary. At Delphi, the famous oracle, a priestess called the Pythia would go into a trance and give a reply which had to be interpreted by priests. It cost a lot of money to consult the Pythia.

The Olympic Games

The Greeks believed that having a fit body was a way of honouring the gods. Games were held all over Greece in honour of different gods or festivals. The Olympic Games were held once every four years in honour of Zeus. They lasted five days, and people came from all over Greece to compete in athletic events. Wars were even postponed for three months so that people could travel safely to see the games. The events included boxing, wrestling, discus-throwing, javelin-throwing, long-jump, running and chariot races.

Important gods

ZEUS and **HERA** were the king and queen of the gods.

POSEIDON was the brother of Zeus and the god of the sea.

DIONYSOS was the god of wine.

ARES was the god of war.

HERMES was the messenger god.

APOLLO was the god of music and healing.

▲ Aphrodite, the goddess of love.

◀ Athene, the goddess of wisdom and of Athens itself, is born from the head of Zeus

Theatre and Writing

Even today, ancient Greek literature is still being read, and plays are still performed.

Poetry was the earliest form of Greek literature. Homer was the first major poet. He wrote long poems telling the stories of the adventures of heroes and gods. His best known poems are the *Iliad* and the *Odyssey*.

The Greeks were the first civilisation to record their history as it happened. Before this, people passed on the news of events by word of mouth and their stories quickly became exaggerated.

▲ In comedies, costumes were padded, making the actors look grotesquely funny.

Drama

Drama developed from songs and dances to honour the gods. Theatres were built next to temples, and plays were an important part of religious festivals. There were two sorts of plays: tragedies and comedies.

Tragedies were sad and violent tales of love and war. They often retold old myths about the gods and related these to the lives of people. Comedies made fun of politics, religion and important local people.

▶ Greek actors always wore masks, which depicted different facial expressions and moods. Wide mouths made it easier for them to project their voices.

At Home

Most Greeks were farmers or craftsmen, living in simple houses. Businesses were family-run with a few slaves to help out.

Greek houses were arranged around a courtyard with an altar in the middle. Ordinary Greek houses were made from mud bricks, dried in the sun. It was easy to dig through the walls, so burglars were known as wall-diggers.

The living rooms were on the ground floor, with bedrooms above. Often men and women had separate living areas and spent most of their time apart. Food was cooked over open fires in the kitchen. The smoke escaped through a hole in the roof.

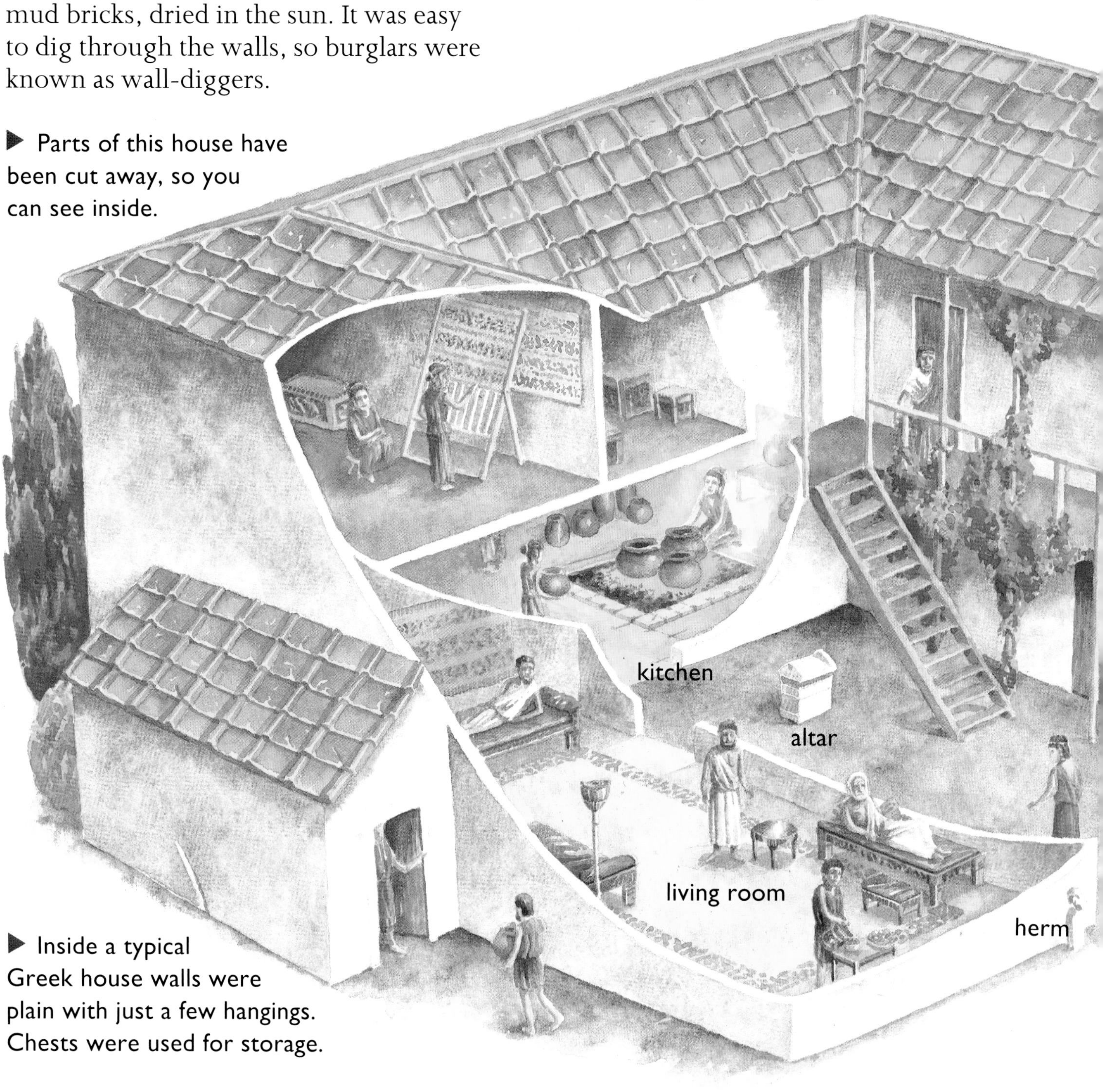

▶ Parts of this house have been cut away, so you can see inside.

kitchen

altar

living room

herm

▶ Inside a typical Greek house walls were plain with just a few hangings. Chests were used for storage.

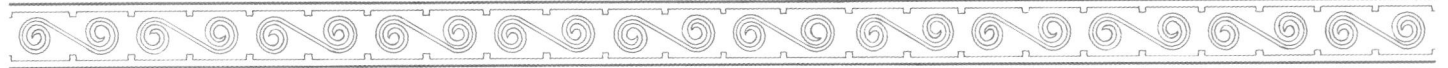

Clothes

Men's tunics were made from wool or linen. A plain square of material called a **chiton** was fastened over one or both shoulders and belted around the waist. Women wore a long tunic called a **peplos**, or a long chiton. Wealthier people had tunics made from decorated material, while slaves had plain tunics. In Classical times, it was fashionable for men to have short hair and a beard.

Cloaks and shawls would be worn outside in colder weather and for travelling. Many people went barefoot most of the time. Shoes were leather sandals or boots.

Although Greek cities always had public baths, there was no soap, so the Greeks rubbed their bodies with olive oil to get clean. Then they would scrape the oil and dirt off with a tool called a **strigil**.

▼ A gold necklace of the sort worn by the woman in the vase painting below.

bathroom

well

▶ A seated woman is adorned with jewellery for her wedding. She wears a chiton sewn up on both sides to cover her arms

◀ At the front of most houses stood a statue of the god Hermes, a **herm**, thought to act as a guard for the house.

Food

The ancient Greek diet was simple and very healthy. The Greeks ate bread, cheese, fruit, vegetables, eggs, and not much meat. Only wealthy people could afford to eat meat often. Many Greeks lived near the sea, so fish and seafood were very popular.

Farmers grew wheat, barley, grapes and olives. Grapes were eaten or made into wine. Olives were pressed for their oil which was used for cooking, lighting and cleaning. Some farmers kept animals such as pigs, sheep and goats. Bees were kept for honey. Vegetables like peas, beans, turnips, garlic and onions were also grown, and fruit like pomegranates, dates, figs and melons.

Breakfast and lunch were small meals, and the main meal was in the evening. Often the Greeks held big dinner parties. Only men were invited and they would sit on couches, eating several courses and drinking lots of wine. After the meal, the men would stay to drink and have a discussion at a **symposium**, or drinking party.

▲ This vase painting shows the messenger of the gods bringing mankind the gift of corn.

Pomegranates

Figs

Fresh dates

Olives

Dried dates

52

Greek Sweetmeats

The Greeks ate **sweetmeats**, made from dates, figs, nuts, sesame seeds and honey, between courses at a symposium, or as little snacks. Here are some for you to make.

Put 100g of sesame seeds into a saucepan with 4 large tablespoons of honey. Ask an adult to help you simmer the mixture over a low heat for 10-20 minutes, until it is a rich gold colour. You can tell if it is ready by dropping a spoonful on a wet plate, letting it cool, then working it into a ball. If it keeps its shape, it is ready. Take the pan off the heat and stir the mixture every few minutes until it is almost cold. Wet your hands with cold water and roll spoonfuls of the mixture into 20-25 little balls. Wrap each sweetmeat in greaseproof paper.

Grapes

53

Arts and Crafts

The Greeks thought that there was a perfect shape for any object whether it was a simple clay pot or a huge temple. They used both mathematics and ideas about what is good in art, known as **aesthetics,** to try to make their art as beautiful as possible.

▲ The Greeks made elegant pots covered in patterns and paintings. Many were used every day, for storing water, oil, or wine, but some of the most beautiful pots were kept carefully and then buried with the dead.

◀ Greek statues were made from stone or bronze. Early statues were not lifelike, but as the skills of the sculptors developed, they became graceful, with expressive faces and clothes which look real. Most stone statues were painted, but have now lost their colour.

► The Parthenon in Athens is one of the finest Greek buildings still standing. It is made from carved blocks of cream-coloured marble, held together with wooden pegs and metal clamps. Each side is decorated with rows of columns, typical of Greek architecture. This Classical style has been copied all over the world. Is there a building like this near where you live?

Bronze Statues

Bronze statues were made with the 'lost wax' method.

 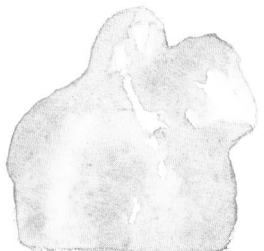 

▼ When the clay was finally removed, a bronze statue was revealed.

Firstly, a clay model was made, and wooden pegs were stuck into it. Then the clay model was covered with a thin layer of wax. The details of the statue's face and clothes were then sculpted onto the wax.

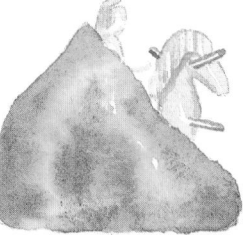 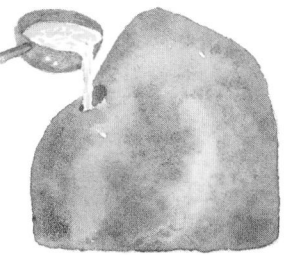

The model was covered with clay and heated so the wax melted and ran out. Molten bronze was poured between the clay layers.

Growing Up

Greek boys went to school from the age of seven until they were 15. Fees were charged, so usually boys from poorer families did not stay at school long. Girls were taught to cook and look after the house by their mothers.

In Athens and many other cities, boys learned reading, writing and maths, as well as music, poetry and sport.

In Sparta, life was much harder. If babies were weak or ill, they were left to die on the hillside. Boys were taught to be tough, to prepare them for their life as soldiers. At the age of seven, they were sent away to a strict boarding school. They had no sandals or warm clothes and had to sleep on the hard ground. They were left hungry and had to steal and hunt for their own food. They were beaten and taught to fight and use soldiers' weapons.

◀ This baby's bottle would have been fitted with a leather or cloth teat.

▶ A child's terracotta doll, with jointed arms and legs.

The Greek Alphabet

Some Greek letters are quite similar to those we use today. You may have heard some of their names before. Do you know where our word 'alphabet' comes from?

Greek letter	Name	English sound		Greek letter	Name	English sound		Greek letter	Name	English sound		Greek letter	Name	English sound
A α	alpha	a		H η	eta	ey		N ν	nu	n		T τ	tau	t
B β	beta	b		Θ θ	theta	th		Ξ ξ	xi	ks		Y υ	upsilon	u
Γ γ	gamma	g		I ι	iota	i		O o	omicron	o		Φ φ	phi	ph
Δ δ	delta	d		K κ	kappa	k		Π π	pi	p		X χ	chi	ch
E ε	epsilon	e		Λ λ	lambda	l		P ρ	rho	r		Ψ ψ	psi	ps
Z ζ	zeta	z		M μ	mu	m		Σ σ,ς	sigma	s		Ω ω	omega	oh

Theseus and the Minotaur

The ancient Greeks told many tales, or myths, about their gods and about the world around them. Myths often included real events from Greek history. This tale recalls a time long ago when Greece was dominated by the island of Crete, and Athens was not yet a powerful city state. It tells the story of the hero Theseus, who overcame the Minotaur, a terrifying beast which was half man and half bull.

Athenians trembled at the very mention of Crete. The name 'Minotaur' was enough to make the bravest man shiver. Every nine years, King Minos of Crete demanded a terrible tribute from the Athenians. Seven young men and seven young women were sent to Crete to be fed to the fearsome Minotaur. A ship with black sails would come to Athens each time the tribute was due. As the ship sailed, a huge crowd would gather at the harbour, weeping and wailing.

In Crete, the prisoners were guests of honour at a huge banquet. They were given fine clothes, and offered the most delicious food. Few of them could eat. Afterwards, they were shut in a large room filled with every possible luxury, but few could sleep.

The next day, they were taken to wooden doors, carved with pictures of galloping bulls. From behind came a loud bellowing and stamping. The doors opened and a prisoner was pushed through.

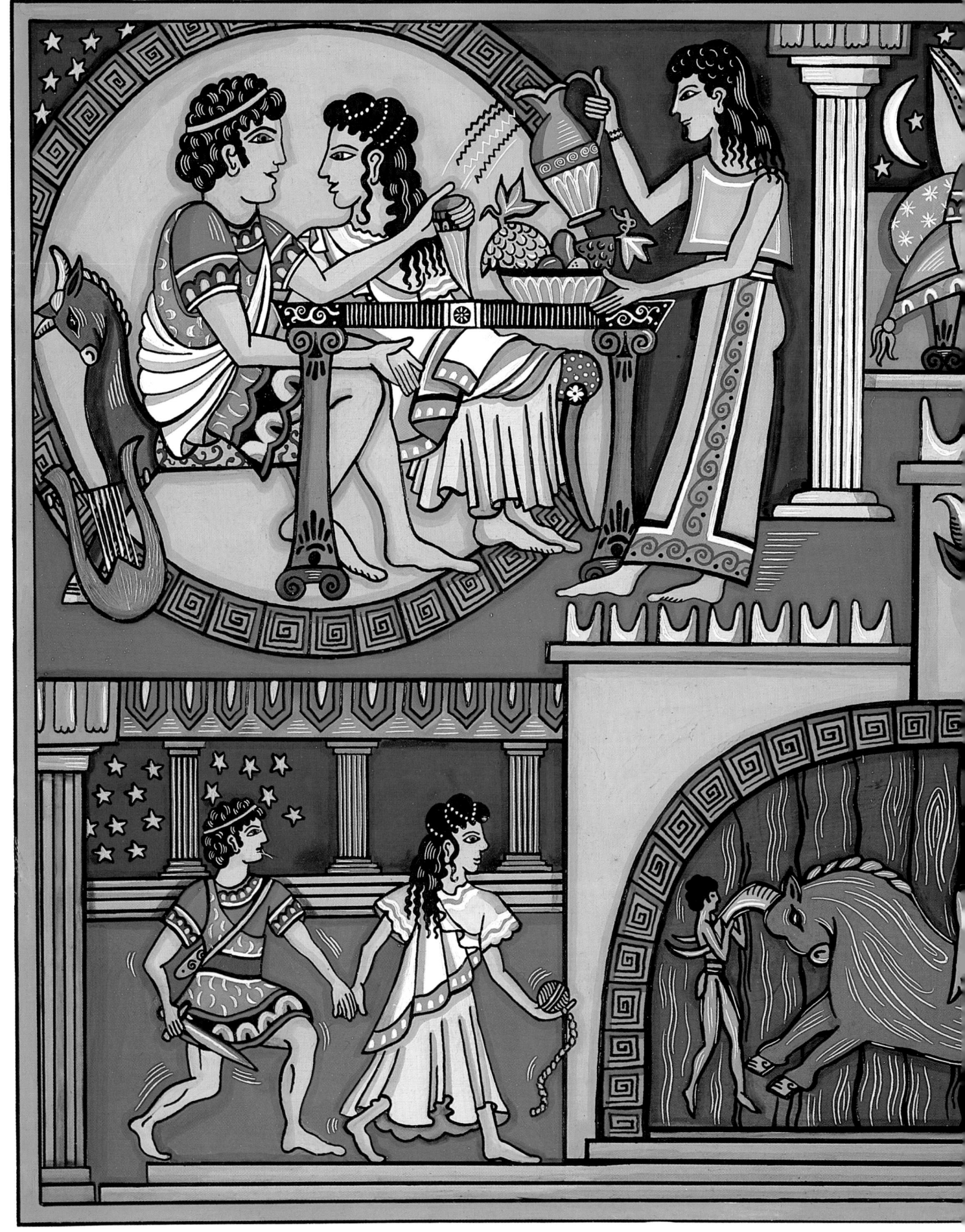

The small crowd of prisoners, guards and priestesses waited until they heard a blood-curdling scream. Then a priestess would point to the next prisoner to be sent through the doors. This went on until the prisoners had all met their fate. Then the Athenians could rest easy for nine years, until it was time to make another tribute.

One year, young Theseus was amongst the people sent as a tribute to Crete. He, unlike the other prisoners, sat dry-eyed on the ship. He laughed and chatted as they prepared for the banquet, until the others began to feel quite cheerful too. At the banquet, he sat near King Minos's daughter Ariadne, who was charmed by this handsome and brave young man. All evening, they sat and talked.

Ariadne told Theseus that behind the doors there was an elaborate maze. Innumerable paths twisted and turned, confusing the eye and the mind. A person entering the maze could never find their way out.

In the very heart of the maze, there lived the Minotaur. He knew all the twists and turns and blind alleys. If someone stumbled into the maze, the Minotaur would find him or her within moments.

Ariadne was determined to help the brave Theseus. After the banquet, she crept into the sleeping chamber and called softly to Theseus. All his weapons had been taken away, but Ariadne handed him a sword. Then she led the way to the great carved wooden door of the maze.

"Here I must wait for you," she said, and she handed Theseus a ball of thread.

"What is this for?" Theseus said, puzzled.

"As you walk through the maze, unwind this thread behind you. If you succeed, you can follow the thread back. The Minotaur will be asleep, so creep silently through the passages until you reach his lair. With surprise on your side, you may beat him."

Theseus took the thread from Ariadne and pushed open the great door. He stepped inside and closed the door, trapping the end of the thread in the crack. Then, holding his sword in front of him, Theseus headed into the puzzling maze. He could hear the snores of the Minotaur, and set off towards the noise. A few minutes later, however, he could hardly hear the noise. The path had doubled back, and he was now further away from the centre than when he had started. Theseus picked up the hanging thread and followed it back to the last place where there had been a choice of paths.

"If I take a path which seems to lead towards the Minotaur, I end up further away," he said to himself. "So, if I choose a path which leads away, I will eventually reach the Minotaur."

So Theseus set off, creeping quietly along a path which appeared to lead away from the Minotaur's snores. Suddenly, he found himself stumbling into the mouth of a dark cave. From inside, he heard a huge roar, followed by the sound of heavy footsteps. The Minotaur appeared in the entrance.

Theseus gasped. The Minotaur was even more terrifying than he had imagined.

It had the body of a huge, strong man, and the head of an angry bull. Theseus picked up his sword, which he had dropped when he stumbled, just as the Minotaur leapt forward to grab him. He struck the Minotaur a terrific blow on the leg. The Minotaur was not used to people fighting back. Most of his victims were prisoners who were resigned to their fate, and did not resist. Within a few minutes, Theseus had struck a terrible blow and the Minotaur lay dead at his feet.

Picking up the end of Ariadne's thread, he retraced his steps through the maze to the outer door. Ariadne was waiting for him.

"Quick," she whispered, "We must hurry. Once my father finds out, he will send all the guards to look for us."

Theseus and Ariadne hurried back to the room where the prisoners were held and told them what had happened. Ariadne distracted the guard while the prisoners slipped out. Then she led them all down to the harbour. They set sail for Athens just as the alarm was raised in the palace.

Theseus was proclaimed a hero by the people of Athens. The Athenians rejoiced that they no longer had to pay their terrible tribute to King Minos.

How We Know

Have you ever wondered how we know so much about the Greeks when they lived so many hundreds of years ago?

Evidence from the Ground

The Greeks built many buildings and made many beautiful objects. Many of these survive but are buried underground. Archaeologists can dig these up and learn much from them. Pictures on pottery, for example, can represent real scenes.

▲ The painting which decorates this plate shows two Greek heroes fighting over the body of a soldier.

▲ Alexander the Great in a detail from a Roman mosaic showing his battle against the Persian Emperor, Darius. Alexander extended Greek territory as far east as India. He brought Greek ideas and customs to all the countries he conquered.

Evidence from Books

The Greeks kept records of all sorts of things, from history and philosophy to lists of goods in stores. Many of these survive, and some were copied out by later people. They tell us all about the Greeks and their lives.

Evidence around Us

Many Greek buildings still stand today as evidence of the skill of Greek builders and architects. Most European languages have words which were originally Greek, especially words connected with the arts, such as 'drama' and scientific words like 'psychology' and 'astronomy'.

▲ The Theseus temple still stands in Athens.

Romans

BRITAIN

Londinium *(London)*

GERMANY

Rhine

Colonia Agrippina
(Cologne)

Lutetia *(Paris)*

Danube

GAUL

ITALY

ILLYRIA

SPAIN

Tiber

Roma *(Rome)*

Carthago *(Carthage)*

MAURETANIA

Mediterranean Sea

The Roman World

Between around 300 BC and AD 200, the people of Rome built up a huge **empire**. It included all of the lands surrounding the Mediterranean Sea and was one of the best-organized empires in history. It lasted for hundreds of years.

Throughout their Empire, the Romans built cities and roads. In the conquered lands, people learnt to live like the Romans – to wear Roman clothes, worship Roman gods and speak Latin, the Roman language. People who had been living in small villages began to live in cities too.

The Romans firmly believed that their own way of life was the best in the world. They thought they were doing the peoples they conquered a favour by showing them the proper way to live.

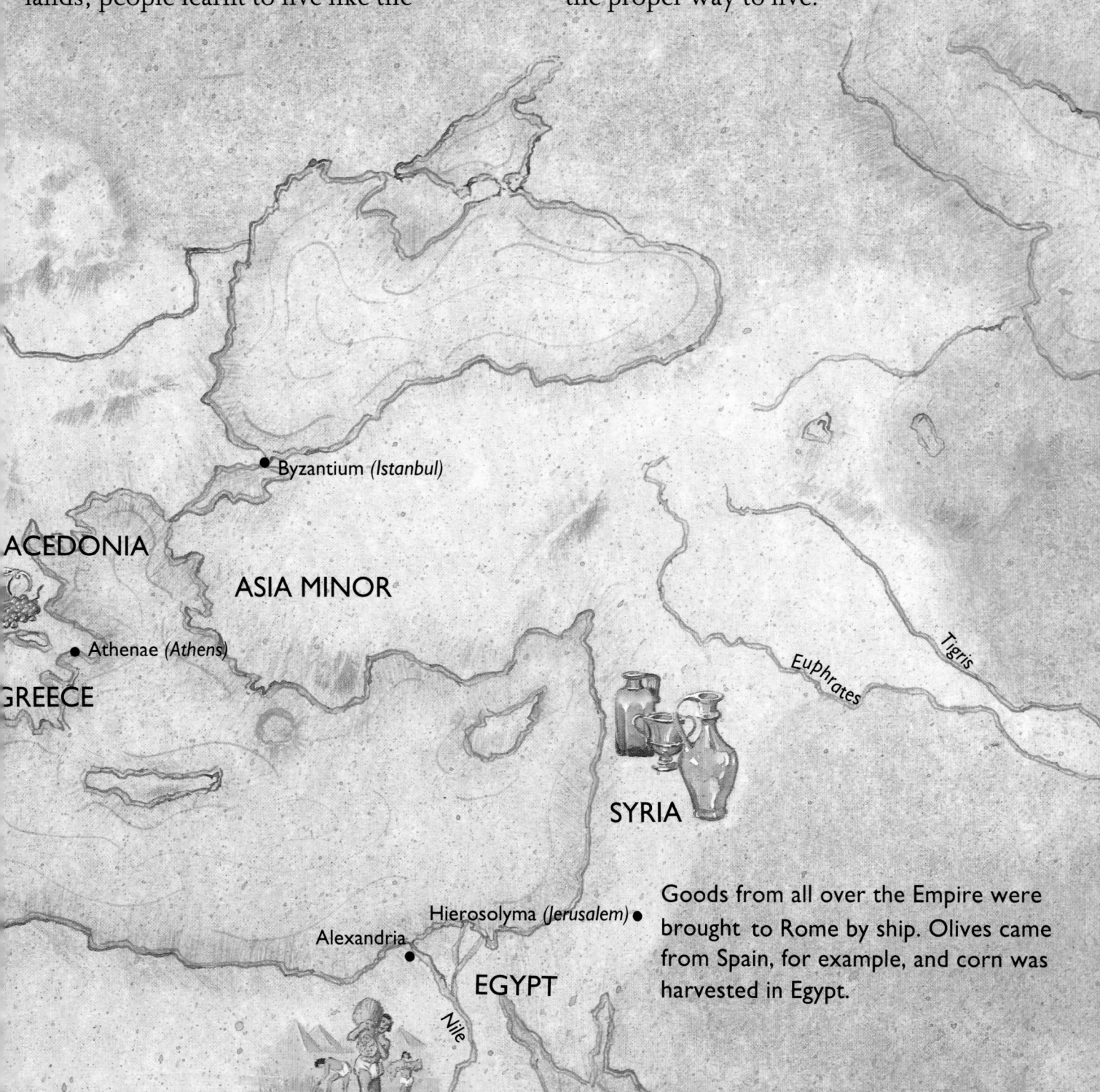

ACEDONIA

ASIA MINOR

● Athenae *(Athens)*

GREECE

● Byzantium *(Istanbul)*

Tigris

Euphrates

SYRIA

Hierosolyma *(Jerusalem)* ●

Alexandria ●

EGYPT

Nile

Goods from all over the Empire were brought to Rome by ship. Olives came from Spain, for example, and corn was harvested in Egypt.

67

The City of Rome

At the heart of the Roman Empire was the great city of Rome, a place where more than one million people lived. For anyone living in the Empire, this was the centre of the world.

The city was full of grand public buildings – temples, theatres, public baths and sports arenas. The streets were lined with statues of Rome's greatest men, and with decorated arches, built to celebrate victories in war.

However, Rome also had many slum districts, where the poorer people lived in overcrowded blocks of flats, separated by narrow, dark alleys.

The Colosseum

Temple of Caesar

The Sacred Way

This is the Forum, as it looked in the first century AD. The Forum was the main centre of government, business, law and religion in Rome. Public meetings were held here and great religious ceremonies took place.

Arch of Titus

Temple of Vesta

Temple of Castor and Pollux

Basilica Julia

▲ The Roman Forum as it looks today. Can you spot the remains of any buildings shown in the drawing?

This is how one Roman writer, called Seneca, described the great capital city where he lived:

'Look at the crowds! They come here from all over the world. Some come for entertainment, others have come to make their fortunes.'

Republic and Emperors

For almost 500 years, until 27 BC, Rome was a **republic**. It was ruled by elected officials rather than by a single person. The most important officials, chosen each year, were the two **Consuls.** They ruled with the advice of the **Senate,** a council made up of men from Rome's most important families.

The republican way of ruling the Empire broke down during a series of terrible **Civil Wars** – wars in which one section of the Roman Army battled against another. The wars were caused by a group of ambitious generals and politicians, who fought among themselves for power.

The final victor in the Civil Wars was Augustus. He made himself more powerful than the Consuls and Senate and became the first of the emperors. These men would rule in Rome for the next five centuries. There were more than a hundred emperors in all.

▼ During the Civil Wars, Julius Caesar, who was a successful general and politician, became ruler of Rome. For five years, he was the most powerful man in the Empire, but in 44 BC he was killed by a group of senators. However, even after Caesar's death, the Civil Wars continued for another thirteen years.

▲ Rome's first emperor, Augustus. Later Romans thought that he was an ideal ruler.

Augustus (27 BC–AD 14)

Augustus was a cautious ruler who gave Rome peace after the bloody Civil Wars. During his reign of more than forty years, the Roman people got used to being ruled by one man. He encouraged the building of many new roads, bridges and temples. After his death, the Senate declared that Augustus had become a god.

Hadrian (AD 117–138)

Hadrian was one of the hardest-working Roman emperors. He spent years travelling all over the Empire, strengthening the frontiers with forts and walls, such as the one he built across northern Britain. When he was not travelling, he was busy changing the laws of Rome. Some of his laws protected slaves from cruel treatment.

▲ These coins show an emperor visiting London, and a new harbour at Ostia, close to Rome.

Coins

Roman coins were not just objects for buying things. They often carried a portrait of the emperor to show people throughout the Empire what their ruler looked like. A coin was also like a small newspaper, announcing great events, such as the building of a new temple in Rome. Other coins praised the emperor's generosity or wise rule.

▲ The Emperor Augustus watches over the building of a new temple in Rome.

The Roman Army

It was thanks to the Army that the Romans were able to conquer and protect their huge Empire. The Roman Army was successful because it was better organized, better trained and better disciplined than any other army of the time.

The Army was divided into **legions**, each of around 5,500 men. Every legion had a number and a nickname, 'Victorious' or 'Lightning', for example. Soldiers were proud to belong to their own legion.

A Roman soldier was a real professional. He would serve in the legion for twenty-five years, living in barracks or a fort with his fellow soldiers. Much of his time was spent training – practising with weapons, or going on long marches loaded with heavy equipment.

helmet with crest

metal jacket

dagger (pugio)

belt (cingulum)

rectangular shield

short sword (gladius)

military sandals (caligae)

▲ An officer's decorated helmet

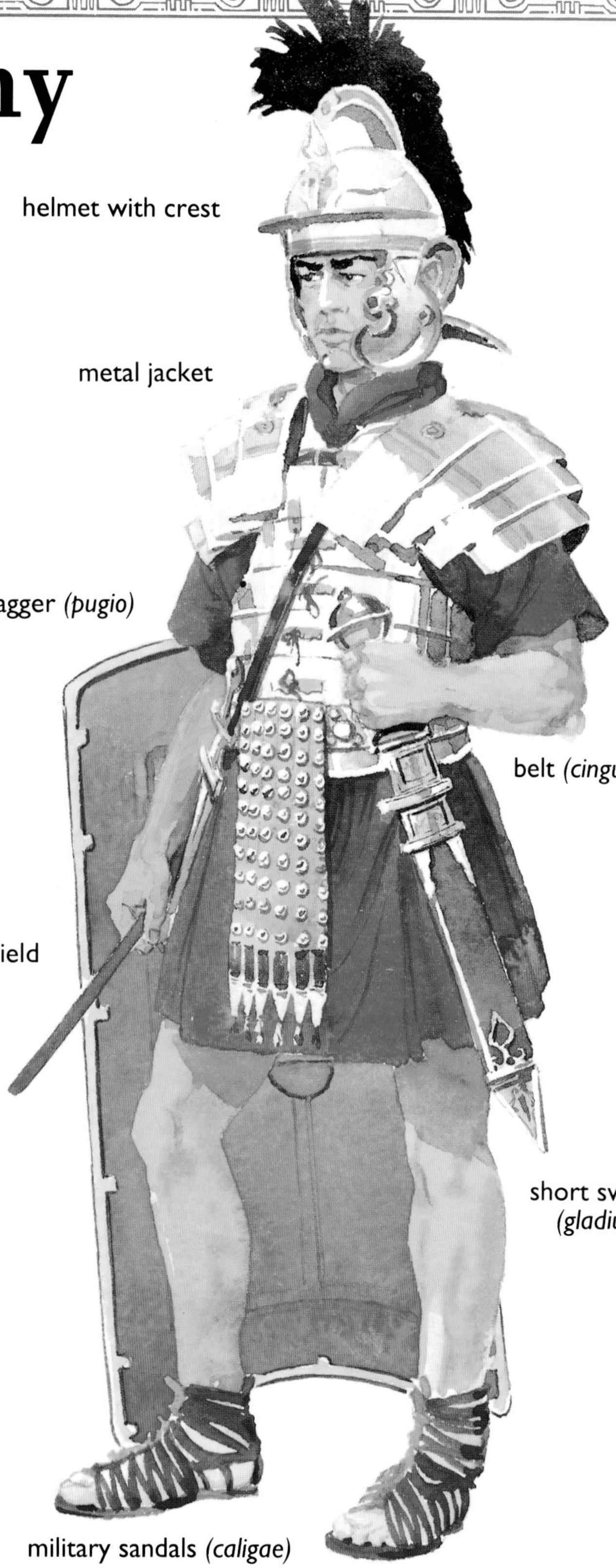

▲ The legionaries wore armour made of overlapping plates of metal, which let them bend freely. The helmet crest was only worn for special occasions such as parades.

72

A Roman Camp

When they were on the march, soldiers would have to build a fresh camp each evening. It would be a rectangular shape, protected by a ditch and an earth bank lined with wooden stakes. Inside the camp, the soldiers pitched their tents in neat rows.

One Roman writer explained the importance of Army camps:

'If a camp is properly built, the soldiers spend their days and nights safe and sound. It is as though they carried a fortified city around with them wherever they go.'

Building Roads

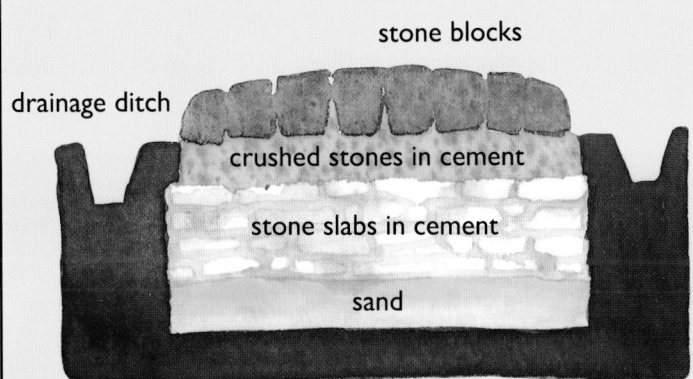

stone blocks

drainage ditch

crushed stones in cement

stone slabs in cement

sand

When they were not training, fighting or marching, the soldiers were kept busy quarrying stone and building roads. These roads were always as straight as possible, so that the Army could travel quickly from one part of the Empire to another. The Romans preferred to tunnel through a hill rather than take the long way around it. However, the ordinary soldiers hated road building and grumbled about it in their letters.

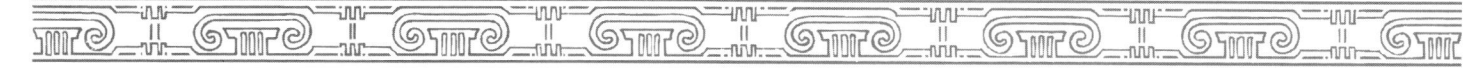

Slaves

Roman society was divided into different social classes. The most powerful people were **citizens**. They were men who had many rights, and could vote in elections.

Slaves were much worse off. They had no rights and were owned by their masters. If they tried to run away they were often whipped, branded with a hot iron, and sometimes even killed.

Many Romans had slaves to do their hard and dirty work for them. These slaves could be bought and sold in the market place.

Some slaves were prisoners, captured in war. Others were the children of slave parents or orphans who had been brought up by slave traders.

Slavery was an accepted part of life in Roman times. Some Romans said that slaves should be treated kindly, but no one thought that slavery itself was wrong.

▼ When rich Romans went out, their slaves would carry them through the streets in a small carriage surrounded by curtains, called a litter.

▲ Slaves often had to wear metal tags in case they escaped. This one says, 'Hold me, lest I flee, and return me to my master Viventius.'

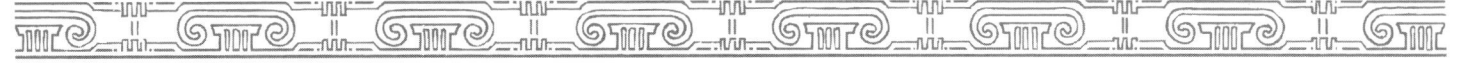

Gladiators

Some slaves and criminals were forced to become gladiators – men who fought to the death in public entertainments.

These fights were hugely popular. The crowds would cheer on their favourite gladiators. When the first blood was drawn, they would cry, 'He's got him!' Gladiators who won fight after fight became as famous as film stars are today. But few of them ever lived to be old men.

▲ An African slave pours a bowl of wine for a Roman. Many Romans were not very tall, and slaves from places outside Italy, such as Germany and Africa, were often bigger and stronger than the Romans. But these slaves still had to take orders from their Roman masters.

Household Slaves

Wealthy Romans had dozens of slaves working in their households. Slaves would help them get dressed, cook for them, entertain them and clean up after them. The most highly-prized slaves were Greeks, for they were often better educated than their Roman masters. They served as doctors, tutors and secretaries.

The Romans came to rely so much on their slaves that they would often treat them as members of the family. Slaves who served their masters well might one day be lucky enough to be rewarded with their freedom.

▲ As well as fighting each other, gladiators were also made to fight wild animals such as lions and bears. The animals were brought to Rome from all over the Empire.

▲ A gladiator's dagger.

Gods and Temples

The Romans worshipped many different gods and goddesses. Each of the gods controlled a different part of life. Jupiter was the most powerful of the gods. His wife, Juno, was the goddess of married women and watched over childbirth.

There were lesser gods for almost every other activity, as well as gods for places, such as hills, crossroads and fields. There was even one goddess, called Cardea, who watched over door hinges!

The most important gods had temples, buildings which housed their statues and which were looked after by official priests. People would bring gifts to a temple to ask the god a special favour. The most highly-prized gifts were the animals that were sacrificed – killed as an offering to the god.

▼ Most Roman houses had shrines. Here the gods who looked after the family would be given offerings of food each day.

▲ The Romans took many of their gods from the countries they conquered. This is Serapis, a sun and sky god, first worshipped in Egypt.

Christianity

The biggest change in Roman religion was the coming of Christianity. The Christians believed in just one god and they refused to worship any Roman gods. At first, the Christians were punished as criminals. But in AD 312 the Emperor Constantine himself was converted to the new religion.

▶ This jug is decorated with Christian symbols.

Signs from the Gods

The Romans believed that they could tell from special signs whether the gods were pleased or angry. One popular way of reading the signs was to examine the liver of a sacrificed animal. Another method was to offer some food to a flock of 'sacred chickens'. If the chickens refused to eat the food, it was a bad sign.

In the third century BC, a general called Claudius Pulcher took the sacred chickens to sea with him. He was so furious when they refused to eat, that he threw them overboard crying, 'If you won't eat, you'll drink instead!' Soon after, he suffered a terrible defeat. The Roman people blamed it on Pulcher's treatment of the chickens.

The Roman Baths

Every Roman town had at least one public bathhouse. Here, for a small sum, people would come each day to exercise, wash, chat and relax.

Men and women bathed separately. The bigger bathhouses had special areas for each sex. In the smaller baths, they would bathe at different times of the day.

Each bathhouse had a courtyard for exercise, such as weightlifting, wrestling or ball games. There was also a swimming pool and a number of rooms which were kept at different temperatures. Bathers sat and sweated in the hot room, where they could also take a hot bath. Then they might move to the cold room for a quick plunge in the cold water.

cold room *(frigidarium)*

▼ The bathhouse needed a large staff of slaves, carrying towels, giving massages and stoking the furnaces to heat the water. The slaves would rub the bathers with olive oil (the Romans did not have soap). Then they would scrape them clean with a curved metal tool called a **strigil**.

▶ Many bathers carried their own oil to the baths in jugs like this one.

warm room (tepidarium)

hot room (caldarium)

▼ The hot room was heated by a **hypocaust** system. Hot air, from the furnace which heated the bathwater, was channelled under the floor and up through spaces in the walls.

hypocaust system

Not everyone was keen on the baths. One Roman writer thought they were a real nuisance, and complained about them in a letter to his friend:

'I live right above the public baths. Imagine the kinds of noise I have to put up with! There are the energetic types, heaving weights about with grunts and gasps. Next the lazy fellow having a cheap massage — I can hear the smack of a hand pummelling his shoulders. Then there's the man who always likes the sound of his own voice, and the others who leap into the pool with a huge splash. And think of the cries of the men selling drinks, sausages and pastries!'

▶ Roman towns used a lot of water, for both baths and houses. The water was brought to the towns along special channels called aqueducts.

Farming

Wealthy Romans were usually the owners of great farming estates. Each estate had a large workforce of slaves, watched over by a steward who was also a slave.

The most important crops were wheat, olives and grapes. Each farm had its own special building for making wine, and presses which crushed the olives to make oil. There were also workshops for the carpenters and blacksmiths, who repaired the farm tools and carts.

Other slaves looked after the cattle, sheep and pigs. The animals' manure kept the soil rich for the growing crops. Oxen were useful for pulling the plough and the cart which took the crops to the market place.

The slaves harvest corn and then thresh it – horses trample on the corn to separate the grains from their husks.

The Romans used pruning knives on their vines and olive trees.

A Farmer's Sacrifice

Throughout the year, Roman farmers had to perform religious rituals. They believed these rituals were just as important as sowing or ploughing at the right time. In May, for example, a pig, a ram and a bull would be led around the boundaries of the fields and then killed as a sacrifice to Mars.

How to Treat Your Slaves

Roman landowners didn't always agree about the best way to treat their slaves. Some people thought it was better to treat slaves kindly:

'The foremen will work harder if they are rewarded. They should be given a bit of property of their own, and mates from among their fellow-slaves to bear them children. This will make them more steady and more attached to the farm.'

But other landowners thought that their slaves were hardly more important than their animals:

'Sell worn-out oxen, worn-out tools, old slaves, sickly slaves and anything else that is no longer of any use.'

▼ This mosaic shows the gathering and treading of grapes, the first stage in wine making.

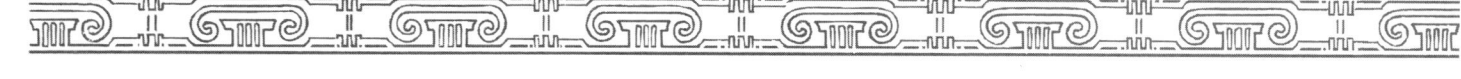

Food

Poor Romans lived on a very simple diet – porridge or bread made from wheat, soup made from millet or lentils, with onions, turnips, beans, figs, olives and sometimes pork, the cheapest meat.

In contrast, rich Romans could afford to buy food from all over the Empire. Different places were famous for their different products – Syria grew pears and Greece produced wine, for example.

A Roman Kitchen

Roman kitchens were usually small rooms, simply equipped. A charcoal fire heated a brick hearth. The cooks fried or boiled food in earthenware or bronze pots. For baking or roasting, they placed meat in the ashes of a small brick oven. The kitchen would also have large jars of olive oil, wine, vinegar and fish sauce, as well as a **mortar** for grinding up spices.

▼ The slaves are kept busy in the kitchen of a rich Roman's house, preparing a dinner party.

◀ Pottery like this was mass produced for Roman kitchens. These bowls come from Sussex in southern England.

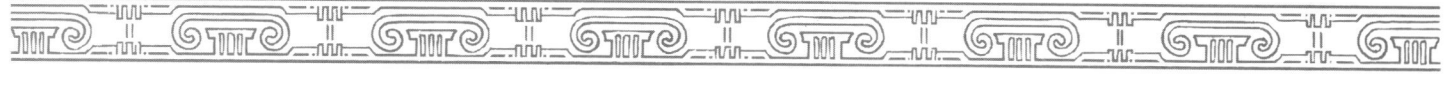

▲ This mosaic shows a slave boy in the kitchen. Can you recognize the different foods?

A Dinner Party

Serving expensive and unusual food at a dinner party was a way of showing off wealth. Guests would eat lying down on couches, leaning on their left elbows while they picked at the food with their fingers. They often had to wash their hands during the meal.

Dinner had a number of courses. It started with an appetizer – salad, eggs, snails or shellfish, such as sea-urchins. This was served with **mulsum**, wine sweetened with honey.

Then the slaves brought out the main courses of fish and meat. Specialities included dormice stuffed with pork and pine kernels, sows' udders and roast peacock – the more unusual the food, the better. Finally there was a sweet course of cakes and fruit.

After the food had been eaten, the guests would often drink more, while they were entertained by singers, acrobats, clowns or story-tellers.

▲ The most popular Roman flavouring was **liquamen**, or fish sauce. It was made from anchovies or the insides of mackerel, which were soaked in salt water and left to rot in the sun. Liquamen was very spicy and salty.

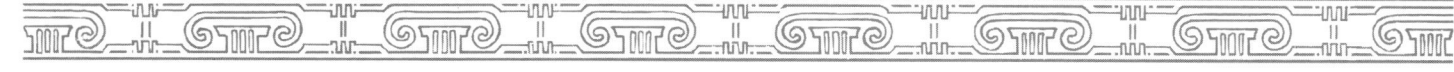

A Roman House

From the outside, the houses of wealthy Romans looked very bare. They were designed to be private and safe from burglary, and so there were hardly any outside windows. Instead, Roman houses faced inwards. Each had a courtyard and a garden, with rooms arranged around them.

If you visited a Roman house, you would first go into the **atrium**, a sort of entrance hall or courtyard – since it had an opening in the ceiling to let in light. Beneath the opening was a basin which collected rainwater. Before aqueducts were built, bringing running water to the houses, this basin would have been the family's main water supply.

From the atrium, you would go into the **tablinum**, a sort of living room and office. This was where the head of the family would greet his daily visitors.

▼ A cut-away view of a Roman house.

peristyle

tablinum

bedroom

atrium

kitchen

Behind the tablinum was the garden, which was full of flowers and ornamental statues. The most popular type of garden, called a **peristyle**, had a covered walkway around its edges, giving shade on hot summer days.

Inside walls were covered with brightly-coloured paintings, showing gods and famous heroes, hunting and farming scenes, landscapes, animals, leaping fish and fighting gladiators. Floors were often decorated with mosaics – pictures made from hundreds of tiny tiles which had been pushed into the wet cement.

▶ A young woman picks flowers in this wall painting. The Romans loved paintings which reminded them of spring in the countryside.

Make a Mosaic

You can make a mosaic yourself, using squares of coloured paper instead of real tiles.

- Cut several sheets of different coloured paper into small squares.

- Sketch the outline of your mosaic in pencil on a sheet of plain paper.

- Then stick the coloured squares in place with paper glue.

- Remember to leave a tiny space between each of your paper 'tiles', so that the mosaic looks realistic.

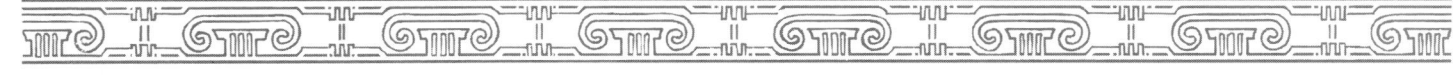

Clothes

Men

Men wore a short wool or linen tunic. Over it, they sometimes wrapped a toga, a big plain woollen sheet, which was arranged in a complicated system of folds.

The toga was rather like a suit today. Men wore togas in public when they were meant to look smart. However, a toga was heavy, and took a long time to arrange properly. Away from Rome, most men normally preferred to wear just a simple cloak over their tunics.

Men were usually expected to be clean shaven. This meant a painful daily ordeal at the barbers, for the Romans did not use shaving soap. Even household slaves would be sent off to be shaved. It was a great relief for many men when the Emperor Hadrian decided to grow a beard and made shaving unfashionable.

▶ A wealthy Roman and his wife in smart dress.

Women

Women wore a much longer tunic which reached down to their ankles. On top they had a stola, a gown belted at the waist, and a broad cloak, often brightly coloured.

Hairstyles for wealthy women were always changing. Hair might be piled up as high as possible, or worn in tight ringlets.

Women also wore elaborate wigs. Some were jet black, made of hair imported from India. There were also blonde wigs, using hair clipped from German slave girls.

◀ Rich women wore beautiful jewellery set with precious stones, such as this necklace, bracelet and brooch.

Romulus and Remus

By the time the Romans came to write down their history, their city was already centuries old. But they told stories about their early years, to explain how their way of life came about. This story explains how the city was founded and why it was called 'Rome'.

Long ago, a wicked king called Amulius ruled over the city of Alba Longa. He had stolen the throne from his elder brother, Numitor, who fled to the hills and hid among the shepherds and herdsmen.

Amulius killed Numitor's two sons and forced Numitor's daughter to become a priestess. That way, she would never marry and have children who might take revenge on Amulius.

Nevertheless, one day Amulius was furious to hear that his niece had given birth to twin boys. She claimed that their father was Mars, the god of war, who had visited her one night in a dream.

Amulius did not believe her and ordered the two boys to be drowned. His servants set the babies afloat on the River Tiber in a reed basket. They drifted towards the Palatine Hill, and finally came to rest under a fig tree.

A she-wolf came across the babies, attracted by their crying. Instead of killing and eating them, she looked after the boys, feeding them with her own milk.

Soon after, an old shepherd called Faustulus was watching his flock when he noticed the fresh tracks of a wolf. Taking his spear, he set off to find the animal and kill it. To his amazement, he found the baby boys, along with the she-wolf, who was licking them clean with her tongue.

Faustulus took the babies home with him and showed them to his wife, Laurentia. The old shepherd and his wife had no children of their own, although they had always longed for some. So the couple decided they would bring up the boys themselves, and named them Romulus and Remus.

The twins grew up among the shepherds and herdsmen of the hills by the river Tiber. As they got older, they showed by their strength and cleverness that they were born leaders. The other boys all respected and looked up to them.

One day, a quarrel broke out between the twins and some herdsmen looking after the flocks belonging to Numitor. The herdsmen accused the twins of stealing cattle. There was a fight, and, in the scuffle, Remus was taken prisoner.

Numitor was puzzled when he met Remus. Something was strangely familiar about him. When Remus told Numitor his age and that he had a twin brother, the old man realized that he was talking to his own grandson! He was overjoyed. He told the twins who they really were, and how his wicked brother had wanted them dead.

Romulus and Remus agreed to help their grandfather get back the throne of Alba Longa. They led their fellow shepherds to the city and made a surprise attack on Amulius, killing him in his palace. Numitor was then welcomed back by the people of Alba Longa as the rightful king.

The twins were now princes in Alba Longa. But they were not happy there. They missed the hills on the River Tiber, where they had grown up. Eventually, they decided to go back there to found a city of their own.

Once they had reached the Tiber, the twins began to argue about where the city should be built. Remus said it should be on the Aventine Hill, but Romulus said they should choose the Palatine Hill, where they had been found by the she-wolf.

At last, the brothers decided to ask the gods to settle the question. Each of them stood on the hill he favoured and watched the sky for birds, signs from the gods. Soon a group of vultures began to circle, high up in the air. Six of them flew over Remus, who shouted, 'Look! The gods have chosen me!'

But then twelve of the vultures flew over Romulus. Romulus began to mark out the boundary line of his city, and his followers started digging a deep trench.

Remus watched with growing anger. He began to shout insults at his brother. For a while, Romulus ignored his brother's taunts, but when Remus and his followers started to jump over the boundary line, Romulus lost his temper. A fight broke out with picks and shovels. Remus was killed.

Instead of showing sadness at his brother's death, Romulus just said grimly, 'That's what will happen to anyone who tries to jump over my city walls!'

The new city was given the name of Rome, in honour of Romulus. He proved to be a wise king, and ruled over his people for thirty-eight years.

One day, while King Romulus was watching his soldiers parade on the Field of Mars, there was a sudden thunderstorm. A thick black cloud wrapped itself around him and, in a flash of lightning, he disappeared. The Romans said that their founder had gone to join his father Mars, up in the heavens.

How We Know

Have you ever wondered how we know so much about the Romans, even though they lived so long ago?

Evidence from Books

The Romans were great writers and many of their books and letters have survived. We can still read Roman poetry, plays and history books, as well as manuals on law, religion, warfare, farming and cookery.

▲ The Arch of Titus in Rome. Since Roman times, many other victorious generals have built copies of Roman triumphal arches such as this.

Evidence Around Us

The Roman way of life still influences our own lives today. Lots of our words come from Latin, the Roman language. Planets and months of the year are still called by Roman names. We use the Roman alphabet too, and many of our buildings, as well as our coins, are modelled on Roman ones.

▲ The scenes on mosaics have told us many things about everyday life in Roman times.

Evidence from the Ground

Many Roman buildings have been uncovered by archaeologists. The most spectacular discoveries were at the city of Pompeii, which was buried by ash and mud from the volcano Vesuvius in AD 79. The remains of the city were preserved for almost 1,800 years beneath the volcanic ash, so that today we can even tell what food was cooking on the stoves when the volcano suddenly erupted.

▲ Many people lost their lives at Pompeii. This boy was buried under the volcanic ash. When his body decayed, it left a space in the ash which archaeologists filled with plaster to make a cast.

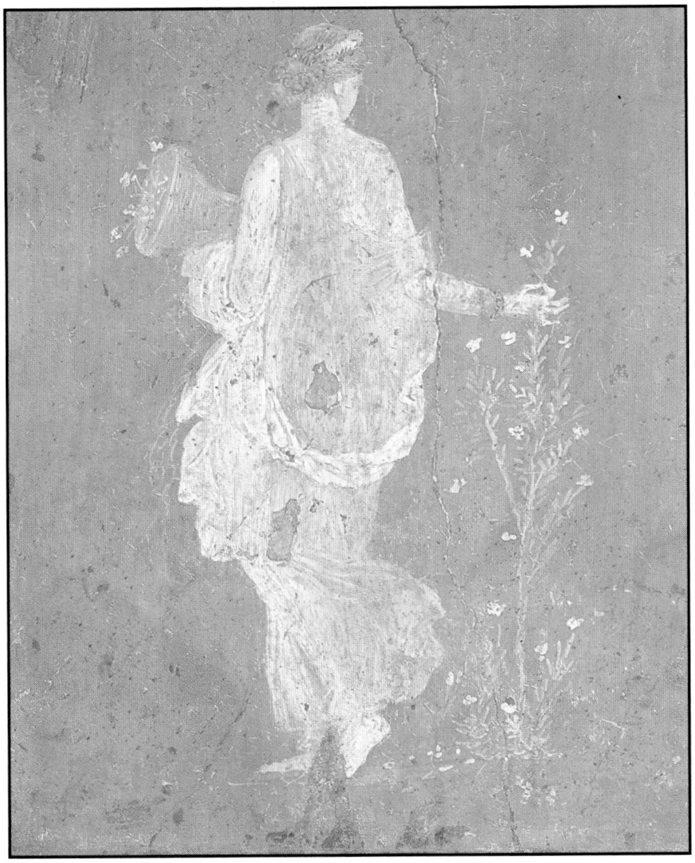

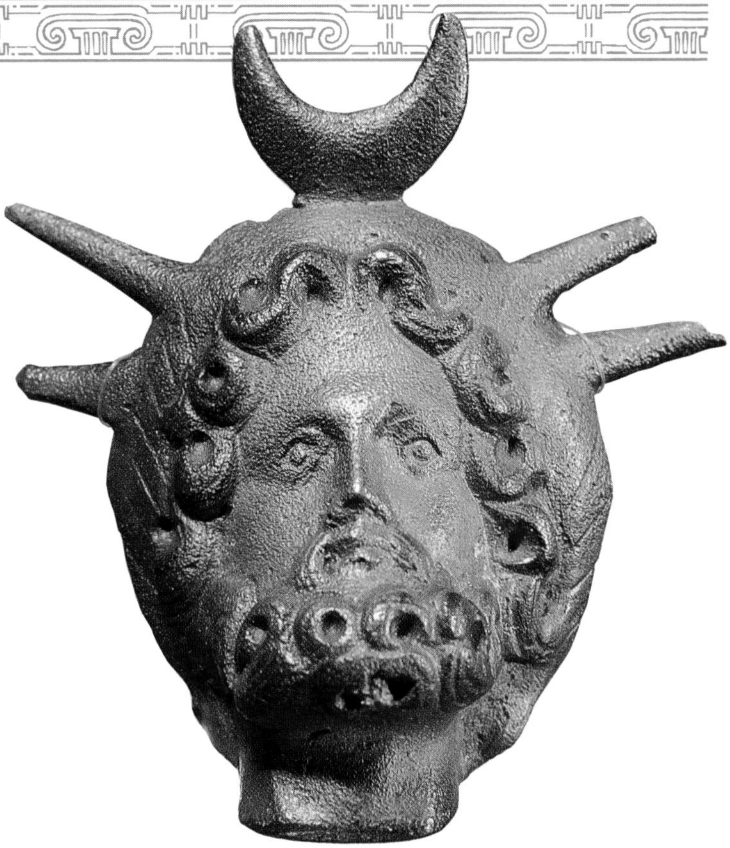

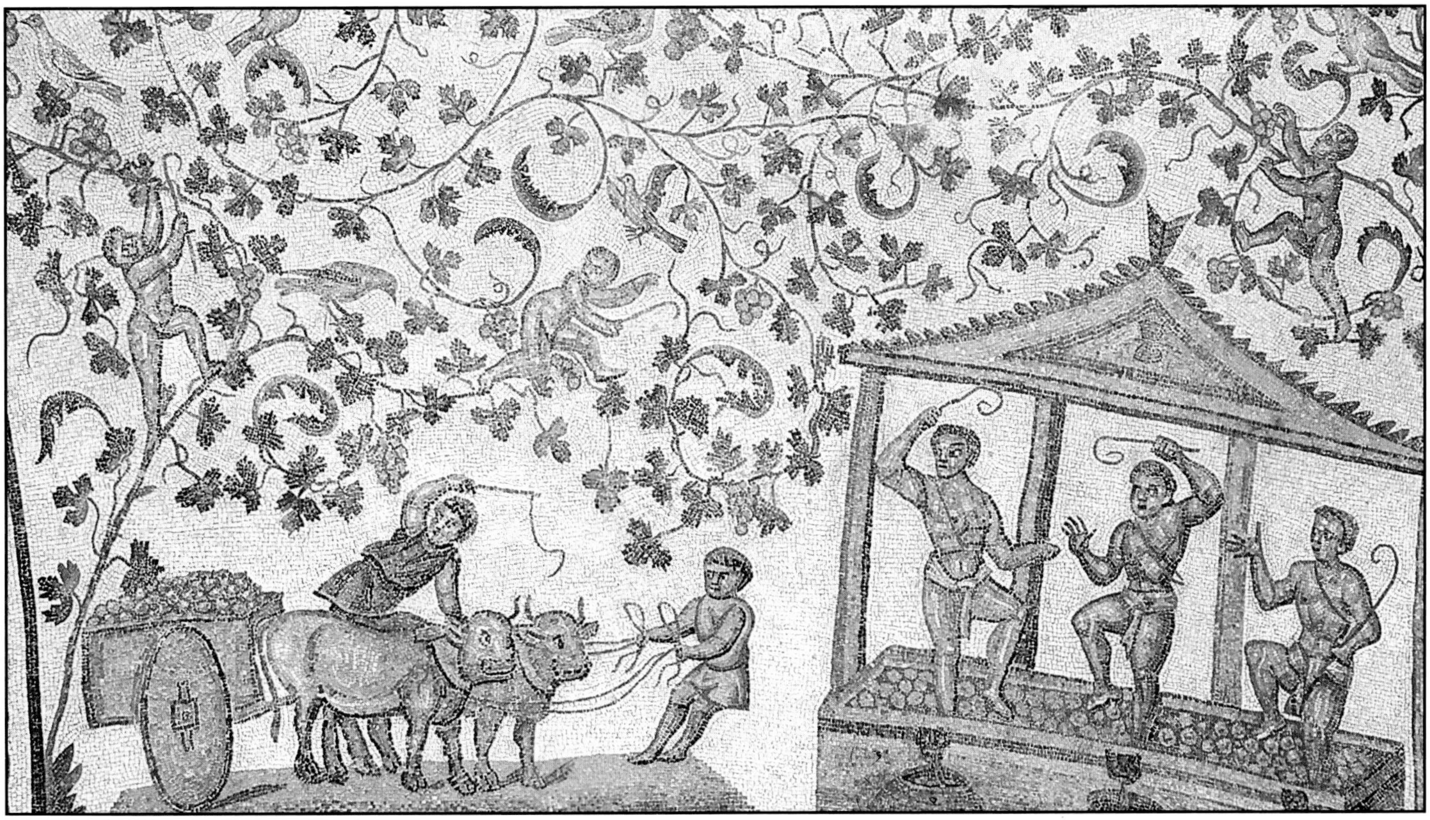

Vikings

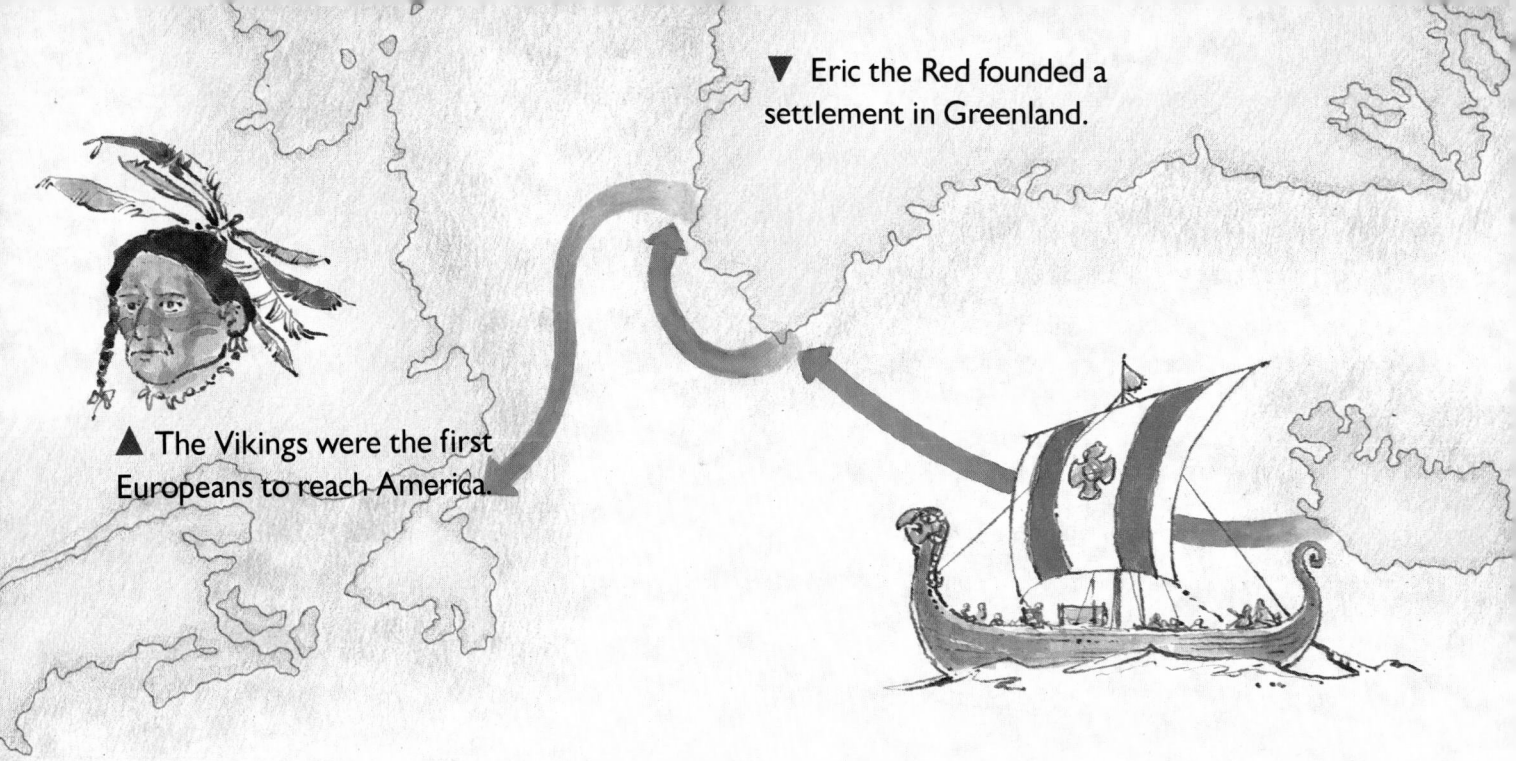

▼ Eric the Red founded a settlement in Greenland.

▲ The Vikings were the first Europeans to reach America.

Lindisfarne was an island whose wealthy, unprotected monastery was an easy target for the Vikings.

"on 8 june the ravages of heathen men miserably destroyed god's church on lindisfarne with plunder and slaughter..."

(ANGLO-SAXON CHRONICLE, 793)

The Viking World

The first glimpse many European people had of the Vikings was when the fierce dragon-heads of the Viking longships appeared off their coasts. No one was prepared for the invading warriors and few countries could resist the Vikings. From the first attacks in 793, Viking raids were a frequent occurrence all over north-western Europe for the next 200 years.

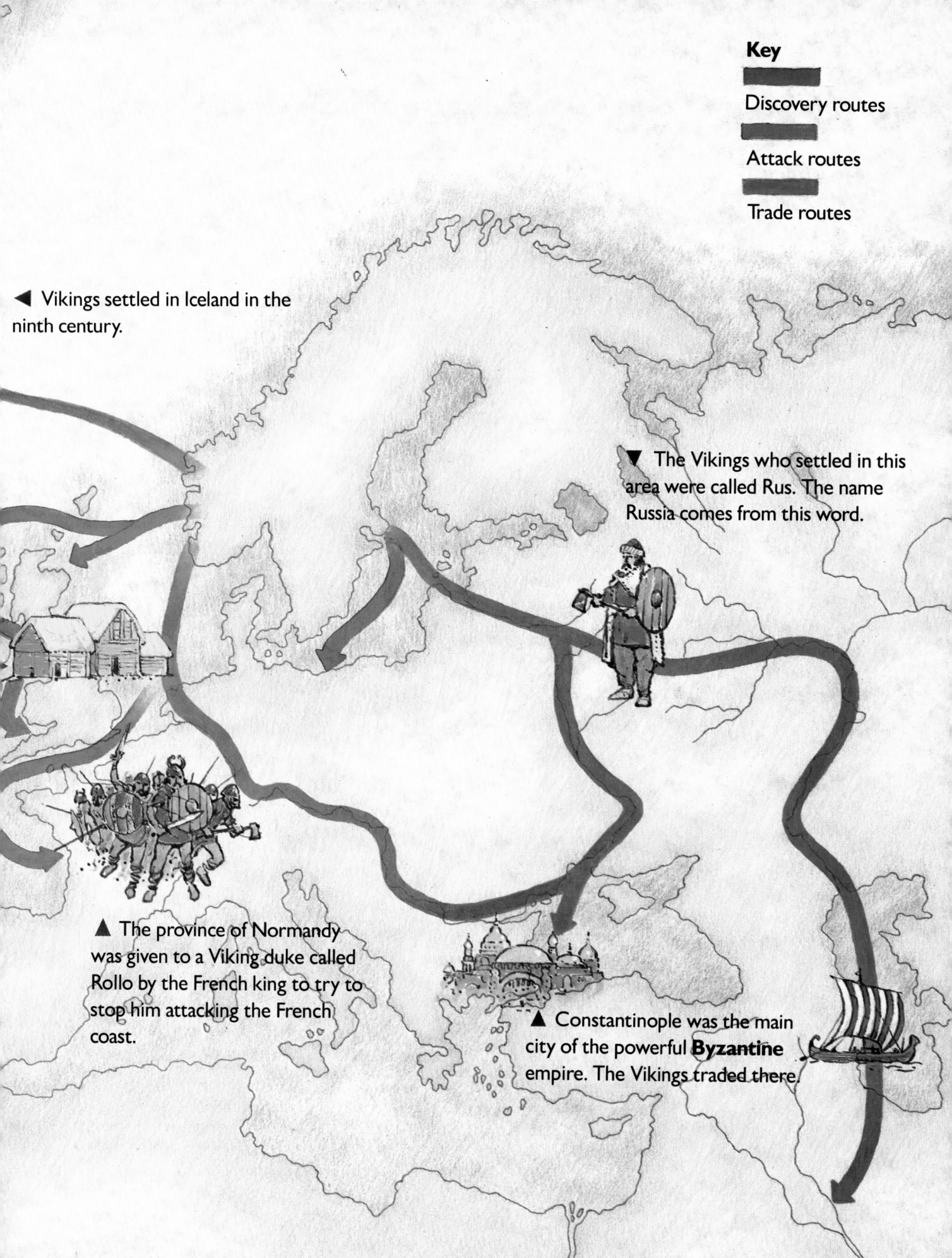

◀ Vikings settled in Iceland in the ninth century.

▼ The Vikings who settled in this area were called Rus. The name Russia comes from this word.

▲ The province of Normandy was given to a Viking duke called Rollo by the French king to try to stop him attacking the French coast.

▲ Constantinople was the main city of the powerful **Byzantine** empire. The Vikings traded there.

Viking Lands

The Vikings came from the countries which are now called Sweden, Norway and Denmark. These lands are cold and bleak, with deep rivers, rocky coasts and mountains. There was not enough good farmland to produce sufficient food for all the Vikings, even though they also fished and hunted wild animals.

Many Vikings chose to leave their homes rather than try to farm the meagre land. They set out to seek riches using their skills as seamen and warriors.

Viking lands were divided into several different kingdoms. The richest and most powerful men became leaders and were called kings and dukes. These leaders would sometimes call all the **free men** to a meeting known as the **Allthing** where they would discuss plans about expeditions to other countries or make decisions about local problems. There were often wars between the different kingdoms, particularly over pieces of good land.

▼ Men gathering for the Allthing.

▼ The narrow, deep-watered fjords of **Scandinavia** form perfect natural harbours.

Pirates or Traders?

Pirates

The Vikings attacked lands around them, particularly Britain and France, stealing food and treasures and carrying people off to become slaves. People who lived in isolated areas on the coast or on islands were terrified of the Vikings' attacks. They were mostly farmers, and were not used to defending themselves and their families. They added to their daily prayers the words "God deliver us from the fury of the **Northmen**."

▲ Viking helmets like this one have been found at a number of gravesites in Europe. Soldiers were often buried with all their weapons because the Vikings believed they would need them on the way to heaven.

▼ Rope was wrapped around the hilt of Viking swords to protect the warrior's hand.

Traders

In certain places the Vikings got food and goods by trading rather than by attacking and stealing property. They usually chose to trade rather than attack when the inhabitants were stronger or more organised and could defend themselves better. Viking traders travelled as far south as the Black Sea trading their furs, jewellery and slaves for spices and wine.

▶ Goods were sold by weight of gold or silver rather than for a number of coins. Merchants used tiny portable scales to weigh the gold or silver. If they needed to give change they would break up the coins.

Longships

The Vikings were superb seamen and used ships for traveling on the lakes, seas and fjords of Scandinavia as well as further afield. The ships were measured by the number of oars they had, the smallest, a **faering**, with 4 and the largest, a **longship**, with about 32. A big longship might be nearly 30 m long and would travel at up to 32 km per hour under full sail. Ships were so important to the Vikings that their language contained dozens of ways of saying "ship".

The Vikings managed to navigate without any of the modern equipment that is used today. They found their way by watching the stars and Sun as well as familiar landmarks such as islands and mountains. They also looked out for birds which are found in different places at different times of year, such as puffins and fulmars.

▲ Viking ships were among the first to have a **keel** which helped them to cut through the water very fast and made them stable even in rough weather.

▲ Oars were used if the sail was not up, when there was no wind or on inland waters. Each rower sat on a box which held his belongings and a waterproof reindeer-skin sleeping bag.

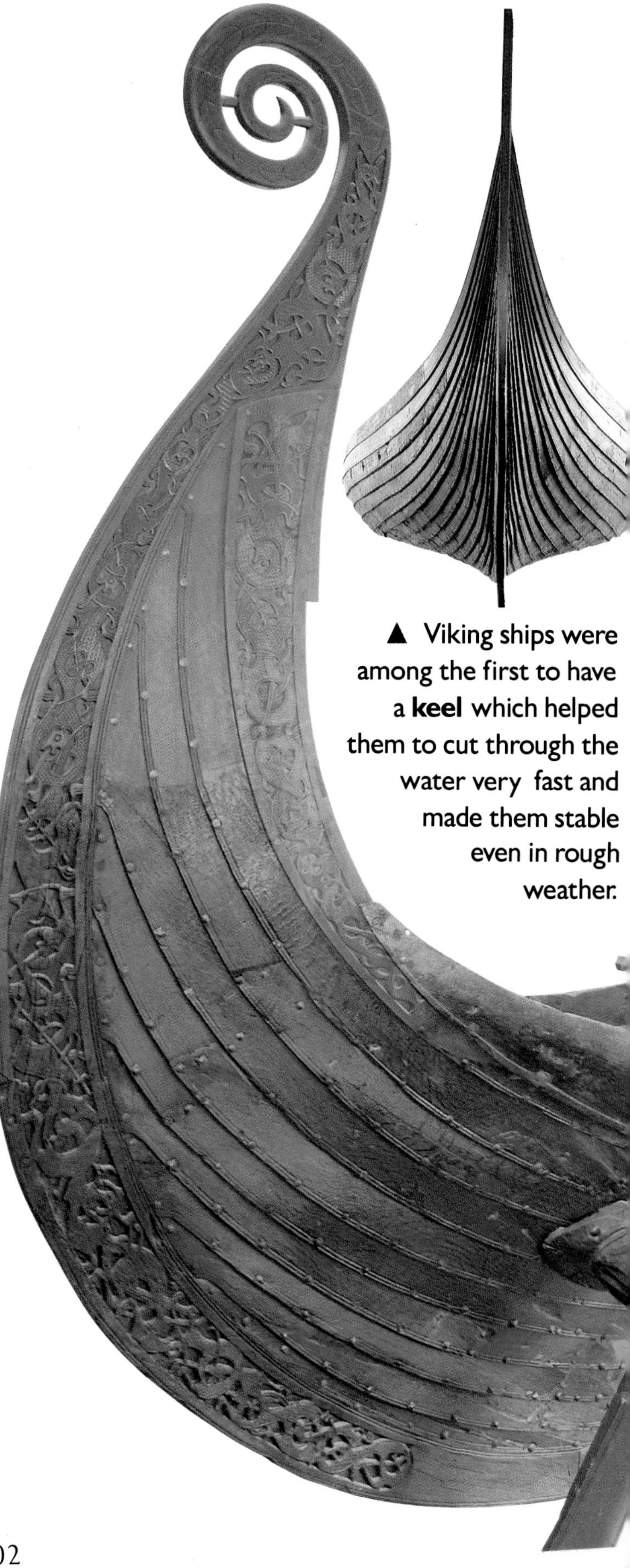

▶ The gaps between the oak planks of the ship were made waterproof by filling them with sheep's wool dipped in tar.

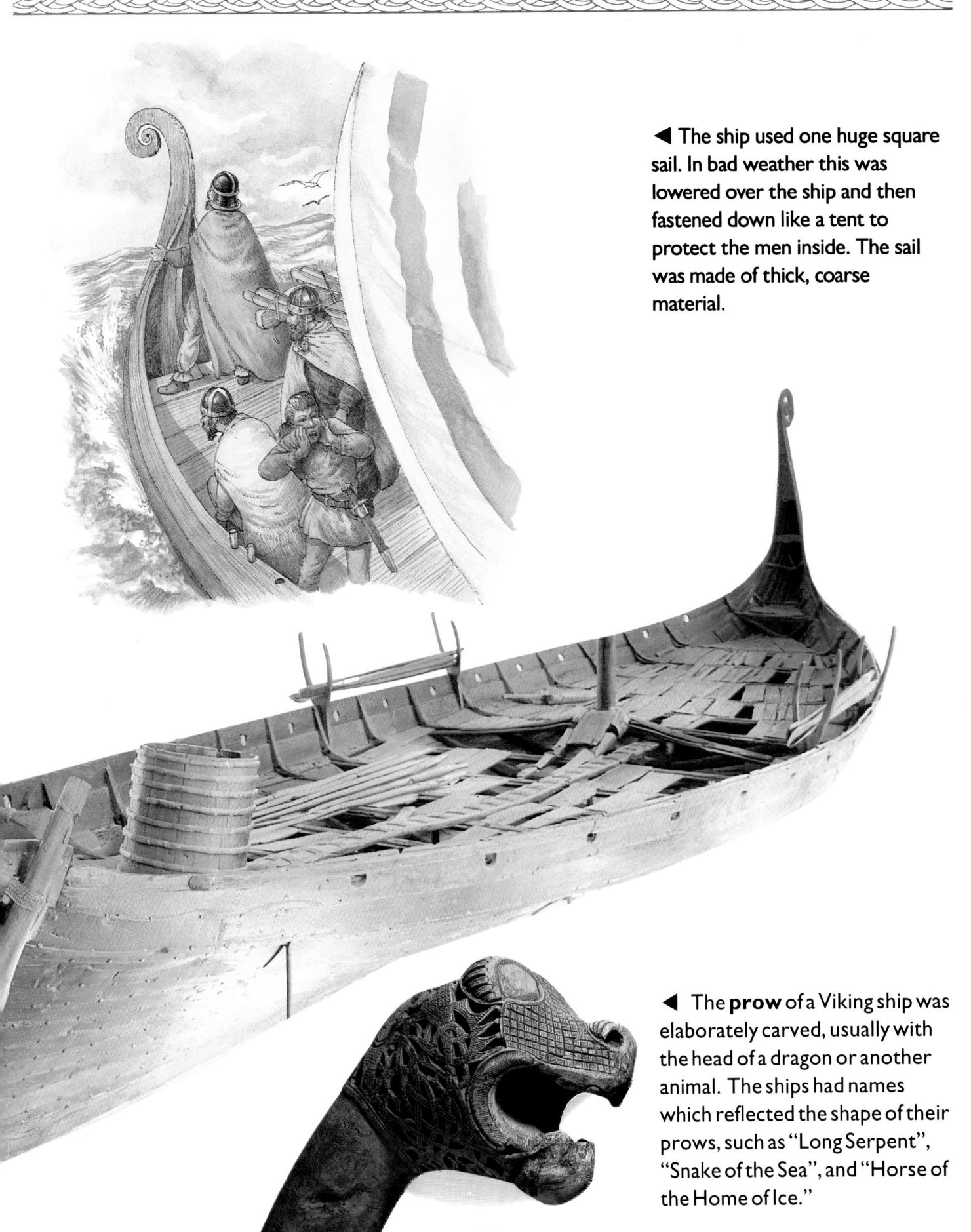

◀ The ship used one huge square sail. In bad weather this was lowered over the ship and then fastened down like a tent to protect the men inside. The sail was made of thick, coarse material.

◀ The **prow** of a Viking ship was elaborately carved, usually with the head of a dragon or another animal. The ships had names which reflected the shape of their prows, such as "Long Serpent", "Snake of the Sea", and "Horse of the Home of Ice."

Heroes

The Vikings admired bold and fearless men and their heroes were all soldiers, sailors or explorers. The deeds of heroes were told again and again until they became more like myths than real historical fact.

Leif Ericson

Eric the Red's son Leif, who was known as "Lucky", arrived in northern America 500 years before Columbus reached the continent. He landed to the south of Newfoundland in a place which he called Markland. He travelled on south to a place called Vinland, which may have been south of modern New York. The Vikings left America after about two years when they were attacked by Indians.

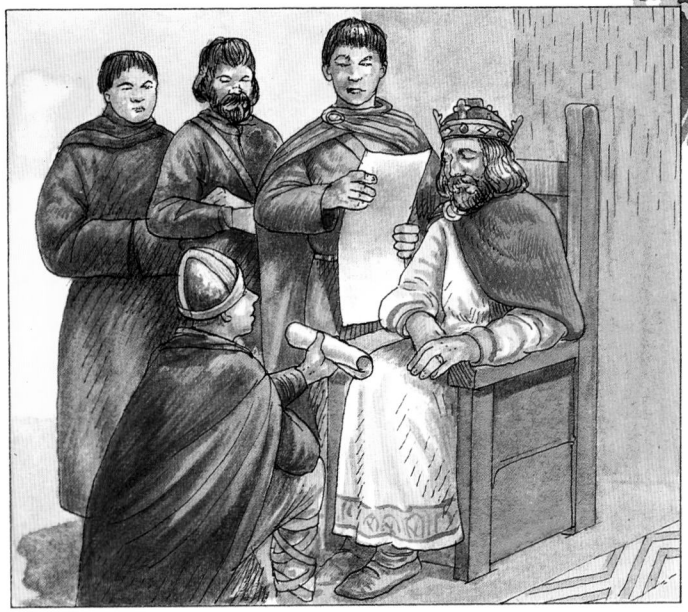

King Cnut

In 1016 England had suffered 200 years of Viking raids, which had made the country very weak. When King Cnut of Denmark attacked England, the English king had just died and so Cnut took over. The English accepted him because he was a wise ruler and brought peace.

Harald Haardraade

As the fame of the Vikings spread throughout Europe, many kings paid Vikings to work in their armies. The Byzantine Emperor had an elite fighting force of Vikings called the **Varangarian Guard.** Harald Haardraade, or Hard-nose, was a famous member of the Guard, who later became king of Norway. He was the last Viking to land with an army in England.

Sagas and Runes

Viking children did not go to school to learn. Lessons came in the form of long stories, or **sagas**, which told the adventures of the gods or of great Viking heroes. These stories were important ways of teaching history, geography and navigation. Children would also learn whilst helping their parents around the house and farm.

Storytellers travelled around reciting sagas at feasts and festivals. They were especially sought after on dark, cold winter nights, when everyone sat inside around the fire.

▲ Some buildings were decorated with pictures from famous sagas. The wood carving above shows Sigurd the Dragon-Slayer attacking a dragon.

▲ This stone carving shows one of the tales of Odin. You can see Odin in the centre at the top, handing a sword to an old man.

The Futhark

The Viking alphabet, the **Futhark**, was quite different from ours. The letters, or **runes**, are made up mostly of straight lines. This is because they were usually carved into wood or stone and it is easier to carve straight lines than curves.

▶ These are all the runes of the Futhark. Underneath you can see how all the letters were pronounced. Try writing your name in runes – it's like a secret code!

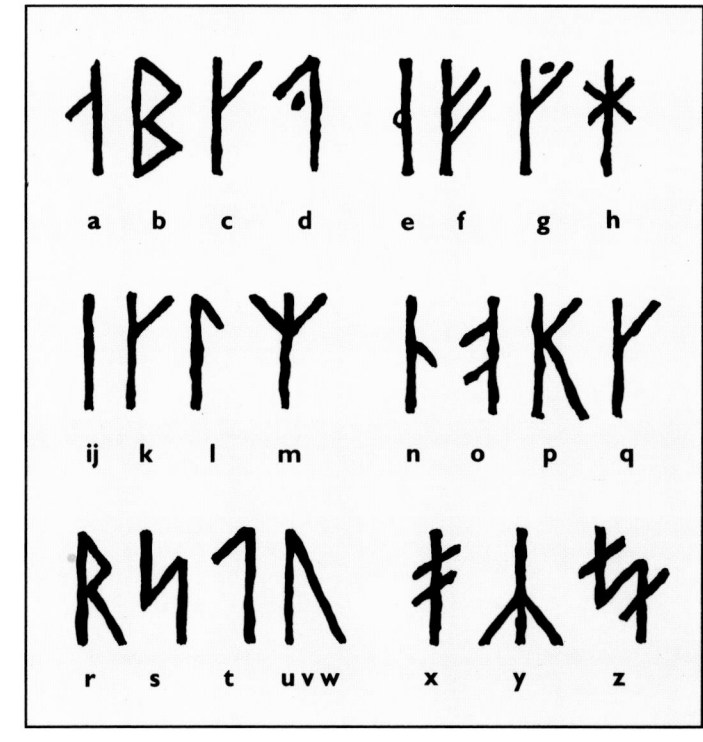

a b c d   e f g h

ij k l m   n o p q

r s t u v w   x y z

The Viking Gods

The Vikings believed that there were lots of different gods who lived in a place called **Asgard**. Each one was responsible for a different thing, such as war, travel or the home. In stories the gods were not perfect. They had very human qualities, and also human weaknesses like jealousy and greed.

If a Viking died fighting it was believed that he went to a hall in Asgard called **Valhalla**, where everybody fought all day and feasted all night.

Some Important Gods

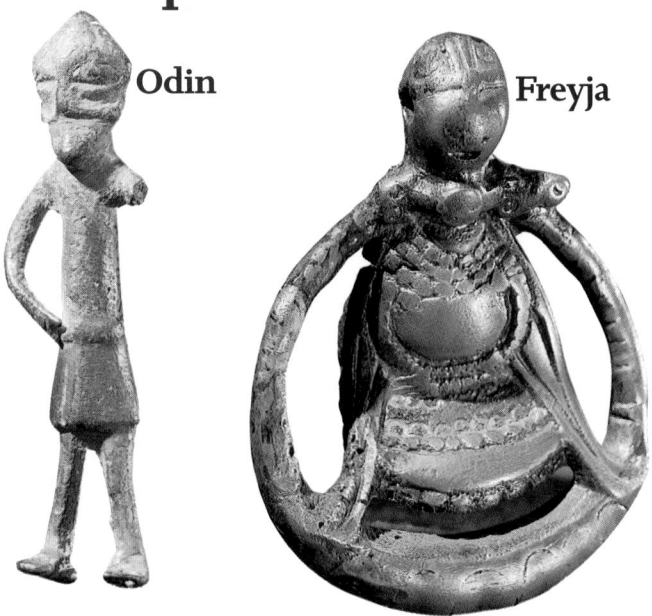

Odin

Freyja

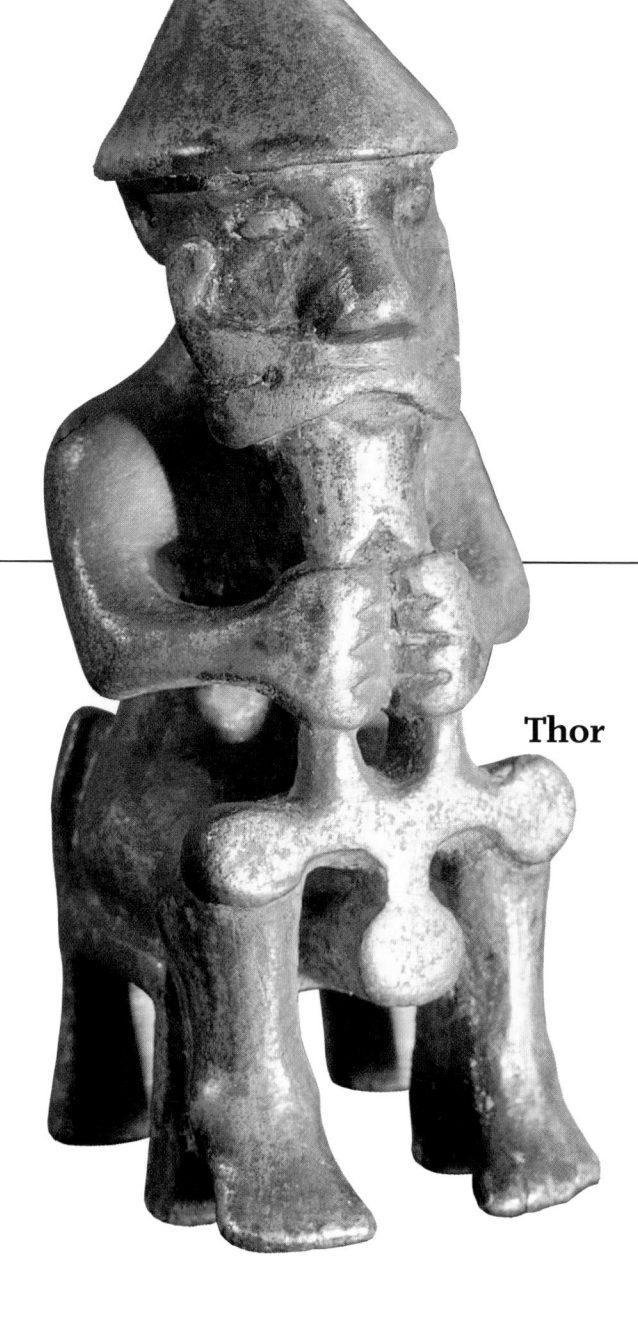

Thor

THOR, the god of thunder, was the most popular god. He was short-tempered and a little stupid, but very good-hearted. He had the qualities that the Vikings thought most important: strength and determination.

ODIN or Woden was the god of war, who rode an eight-legged horse. He often doubted himself and spent too long trying to decide whether to do things or not.

FREY made sure that the sun shone, rain fell and the crops grew. He owned a magic boat which could carry all the gods at once, but folded up in his pocket when not needed.

FREYJA was Frey's sister. She was the goddess of love and war. She could turn herself into a bird by putting on a magic falcon-skin.

LOKI was half god, half fire-spirit. He caused the other gods a lot of trouble.

▲ When Viking warriors died
their bodies were often placed in
longships, which were buried or
set alight and pushed out to sea.

► Towards the end of the
Viking age the Vikings began to
convert to Christianity. This is a
mould made in the tenth century
for making Christian crosses, but
it could also be used for making
copies of **Mjollnir**, Thor's hammer.

At Home

The Vikings were not only skilled soldiers, seamen and traders. Most Vikings were farmers and lived with their families, growing and making all the things they needed for their daily lives. Children helped their parents as soon as they were able to. Even very small children had their own jobs around the farm, like feeding the animals or gathering firewood.

Viking women worked on the farm and wove material for clothes and blankets on small looms. When their husbands were away fighting, they took care of the whole farm.

Viking houses were made of timber planks and woven branches, with turf or thatched roofs. Stone was used in places where there was no wood, like Shetland and Iceland. Inside, the houses were not divided into rooms. Areas were separated off by stretching cloth or skins between the pillars which supported the roof.

A typical farm would contain the family house, or more than one house if the family was large. There were also sheds for the animals, a workshop with a furnace for making metal tools, and small huts for slaves.

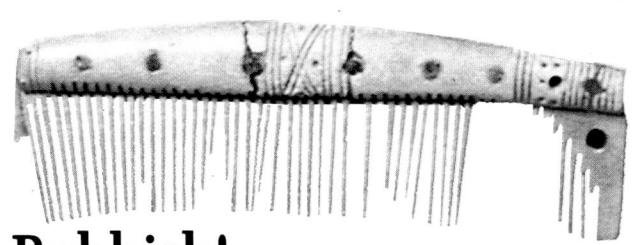

Rubbish!

● Viking homes were not as clean as our houses are. Meat bones and vegetable peelings might be left on the floor all winter and only cleared out in the spring.

● Rubbish was buried outside.

● All the Vikings had combs because they had lice in their hair.

Games

Viking children did not spend all their time helping their parents. They had some time to themselves for playing games and carving wooden toys. Girls and boys went skating in winter, using skates made of carved bone. These were strapped to the children's shoes with strips of leather.

When it was too dark and cold to go outside, Viking children may have played a game called **hnefatal**. This was a board game rather like chess but with simple pieces, like draughts.

Crafts

Vikings were very skilled craftsmen, making marvellous objects from stone, wood and metal. Many of the most beautiful objects were not made by specialist artists, but by ordinary people. A farmer might make a brooch using the same furnace he used to make his plough.

As there were no banks, people wore their wealth in the form of jewellery. This was the best way to keep it safe.

Smiths were very highly respected and often became very wealthy. Thor, one of the most important Viking gods, used a smith's hammer as his main weapon.

▲ Some jewellery was made specially for burial with a dead person. This arm-ring was found at a burial site.

Make Some Viking Jewellery

Look at the decoration on the Viking objects in this book. Can you see how all the figures are woven around one another? The Vikings loved to use complicated patterns for decoration.

Try making a bracelet or brooch using Viking designs. Modelling clay that you can bake hard in the oven is good for making jewellery.

◀ Use four balls of clay to make the heads.

▼ Roll out three long strands and plait them together.

▼ This is a mould which was used to make part of a helmet. Once the mould was made, many helmets could be made with this pattern.

▶ This gold pendant was worn around the neck as a magical amulet. Look at the elaborate patterns that cover it.

▶ The symbol of Thor's hammer was used in much Viking jewellery. This hammer head is made in silver but many were much simpler than this.

Food

Finding food was a very important part of a Viking's life. Little of the land was fertile and the winters were very long and harsh, so as well as growing and raising food on their farms, the Vikings hunted and fished for food. They ate rich stews of beef or mutton from their farms, or fish and whale meat. They grew vegetables like cabbage, peas and beans and also ate wild leeks and garlic.

Trestle tables would be set up in the middle of the room for meals, and members of the family would sit on the same wooden benches that they slept on at night. They ate off rectangular wooden platters or from soapstone bowls, using spoons and the knives that were carried on their belts at all times.

The Vikings used drinking horns as well as cups. Because the horns did not have flat bottoms, they had to be passed on around the table until they were empty. A man who could drain a drinking horn at one go was very highly thought of! The usual drink was mead, a sweet beer made from honey.

Food Facts

- When the Vikings had no other grain they would use peas to make bread.
- Salt was made by boiling sea-water.
- The Vikings ate two meals a day: the **day meal** after the early farmwork and the **night meal** at the end of the day.

▼ Cooking was done over an open hearth fire. Meat was roasted on huge spits, and stews were made in big iron cauldrons. Sometimes a **gridiron** made of coiled iron was used. Does it remind you of part of a modern cooker? Bread was baked in stone ovens or in the ashes of the fire.

▼ Bowls were made from pottery or soapstone.

Clothes

Most Viking clothes were made from coarse woollen cloth, although some rich people wore imported silk or linen. In winter people wore furs to keep warm.

Men wore an undershirt and breeches, covered by long woollen trousers and a tunic which reached to the knees. All this was held up with a leather belt. A purse and knife were carried on the belt.

Women wore long wool or linen dresses with a woollen tunic rather like an apron attached with brooches. Hanging from their belts they carried a knife and keys.

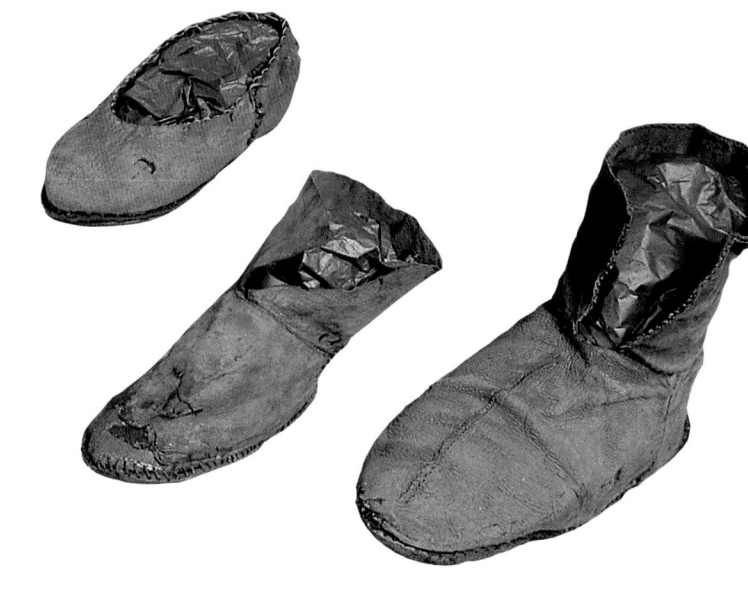

▲ Shoes were made from leather or goatskin, laced up with strips of leather.

Thor Visits the Land of the Giants

This story is part of a Viking saga. It is about Thor, the god of thunder, and the journey he set out on to prove his strength. The journey and the trials of strength would have been very familiar to the Vikings.

One summer day, Thor, Loki and their two servants set off to visit Utgard, the land of giants. After a long journey, they arrived at the gates of Utgard to find them locked. Thor thumped and hammered on the gates, calling out for someone to come and let them in, but Loki grinned and slipped through the bars, dragging the others after him. They walked into the great hall of Utgard. In the middle of the hall was a long table around which hundreds of giants were seated on benches, eating and drinking and making the most enormous noise. The giants all began to laugh as Thor marched up to the Giant King who was seated on a chair at the far end of the hall.

"Greetings, Giant King," said Thor, politely.

The Giant King sat chewing bones and did not even look at Thor. From time to time he tossed a bone over his shoulder and picked up a new one.

Thor spoke again, a little louder: "Greetings, Gi . . ."

The Giant King interrupted: "So you're the great thunder god Thor, are you? Well, you look like a scrawny little piece of work to me. I suppose you've come to test your strength?"

Thor was furious at the Giant King's rudeness, but it did not seem a very good idea to lose his temper when he was surrounded by giants.

"What skill would you like to challenge us with?" continued the Giant King.

Thor looked around him at the giants.

"I doubt if anyone here can drink as much as I can," Thor replied.

The Giant King signalled to a servant, who brought forward a huge drinking horn.

"This is the horn used by all my followers," he said. "A good drinker can finish it in one draught, and all here can down it in two at the most. Let us see what the great Thor can do!"

Thor took the horn. It was certainly not the largest he had ever drunk from. He raised it to his mouth and began to swallow. He felt sure he could drink it all, but he ran out of breath before the horn was empty. He looked into the horn and found that it was no less full than before. He drank a second time, and again had to stop for breath. This time the horn was no longer brimming full. He took a third draught, gulping down the liquid until he was sure he must empty the horn, but although the level was lower than before, the horn was by no means empty.

"You don't seem to be much of a drinker," said the Giant King. "Why not try your strength? Some of the younger giants like to test themselves by lifting my cat. We don't think this much of a feat, but perhaps you'd like to try?"

Standing beside the Giant King's chair was the most enormous cat Thor had ever seen. He braced himself and then put both arms under the cat and heaved. The cat simply arched its back. Thor heaved again and managed to make the cat lift one paw off the ground before he had to admit defeat.

"As I thought," said the Giant King scornfully. "You may be strong in Asgard and in the realms of men, but your strength is nothing here."

At this Thor grew angry. "I can match any of your men in a fight. Just let anyone here wrestle with me."

There was a roar of laughter from all the giants in the hall.

"Everyone here feels that wrestling with you would be too easy," said the Giant King. "Perhaps you could fight Elli, my foster mother."

A wrinkled old woman hobbled forward leaning on a stick. Thor thought that the Giant King was making fun of him until Elli threw down her stick and took hold of him. He knew at once that his strength would be sorely tested. They struggled and fought, but eventually Elli threw Thor off balance so that he landed on one knee.

"Enough, enough!" shouted the Giant King. "You have shown us that you have no strength as a wrestler either. As you pose no threat to us, you may eat with us and spend the night here in Utgard."

Thor and his companions were very hungry and tired after their long journey. When they had eaten, the tables were pushed back, and they spread their bedding in a space on the floor among the giants.

Thor awoke early, before any of the giants, and roused his companions.

"Come, let's go before the giants wake up," he whispered.

They tiptoed over the sleeping giants and out of the gates of Utgard. To their surprise, they found the Giant King already outside waiting for them. He walked with them across the plain for a while.

At last he stopped: "This is where I must leave you. Thor, do not feel too badly about your failures last night."

Thor was puzzled. "But I have never before been so soundly beaten," he said.

The Giant King replied: "You were not competing in a fair fight. I feared your strength, so I used magic to deceive you. The other end of the horn that you drank from was in the sea. When you reach the shore you will see just how much you have lowered its level. The cat you lifted was really the giant serpent whose body is wrapped around the world. You managed to lift it until its back touched the sky. And as for Elli, it was a wonder you withstood her for so long. You see, Elli is Old Age, which defeats all men in time."

Thor was furious that he had been tricked. He seized his hammer Mjollnir and swung it around his head, but the Giant King and Utgard had vanished, as if they had never been.

How We Know

Have you ever wondered how, although the Vikings lived over 1000 years ago, we know so much about their daily lives?

Evidence from the Ground

Certain objects have been found preserved in wet earth or water. Often these are very ordinary objects which were thrown away by the Vikings because they were broken or not needed. Archaeologists piece them together and work out how the Vikings used them.

Some important Vikings were buried in ships full of their possessions. When these ships are discovered, archaeologists can gain a lot of information about the Vikings.

Evidence from Books

Many of the stories told by the Vikings were written down, and so it is quite easy to find out who the important gods were and what various historical figures did. We even know that when Eric the Red discovered Greenland, he gave it that name in spite of its cold iciness because "many would want to go there if it had so promising a name".

Evidence around us

Many place names in Europe were originally Viking names, and so we can tell where the Vikings settled.

The whole of Normandy in France was taken over by the Vikings, and the name means land of the Northmen.

In Britain many place names have the Viking endings "-thorpe" and "-by", like Scunthorpe and Grimsby. Can you find any others on a map?

And what about our days of the week? Did you know that Wednesday was originally Woden's day, and Thursday Thor's day?

Glossary

Absolute ruler An Egyptian ruler who can make laws without consulting any other person or group of people.

Aesthetics Ideas about what is good in art. The Greeks believed that balance and symmetry were very important in art.

Akhet An Egyptian word used for the yearly flooding season on the Nile.

Allthing A council of free men which met when problems arose. This was the only form of government the Vikings had.

Asgard The place where the Vikings believed that their gods lived, and where they would go when they died.

Atrium The entrance hall of a large Roman house.

Byzantine The strongest world power at the time of the Vikings was the Byzantine Empire in the east, which lasted from the 6th to the 15th century.

Chiton A simple tunic worn by men and women in Ancient Greece.

Citizen A citizen in Ancient Greece was a person who had the right to own property and take part in politics and law. **Roman citizens** – people who lived in the city of Rome – were members of a state and had more rights than people who lived in the Empire outside of Rome. Only Roman citizens could stand for election, vote and join the Army.

Civil war A war fought between people who belong to the same nation.

Civilisation An organised society which has developed social customs, government, technology and the arts.

Consuls The two most important officials in the Roman government under the Republic.

Day meal The first meal of the day for Vikings, eaten after the farmwork was done.

Democracy A political system involving government by citizens. In Greece, only those who owned property were entitled to be citizens, with the right to vote on matters of government.

Demotic A form of ancient Egyptian writing, developed from 700 BC onwards, and used for business and administration.

Empire A large area with many different peoples, all ruled by a single government.

Faering The smallest type of Viking ship, with four oars.

Free men All the men who were not slaves. Slaves were usually people who had been captured on Viking raids.

Futhark The runic alphabet used by the Vikings. The word is taken from the sound of the first six letters.

Gridiron A coiled metal strip which was placed in the fire by Vikings to heat pots on.

Herm A small statue which stood outside the door of a Greek house which was thought to protect the household.

Hieroglyph Symbol used in ancient Egyptian writing standing for a word or group of letters.

Hnefatal A Viking board game.

Hypocaust A type of central heating, using hot air channelled under the floors, which were held up on brick columns.

Inundation The yearly flooding of the Nile valley in Egypt.

Julius Caesar Roman general who became leader of the Roman Empire.

Keel The long timber which forms the lowest part of a ship and helps it to balance.

Legion A division of the Roman Army, made up of around 5,500 men.

Liquamen A popular Roman sauce made from rotten fish.

Longships The long, low ships used by Vikings.

Mark Antony The Roman general who married Cleopatra VII.

Mjollnir Thor's hammer in Greek mythology. He was said to have carried it with him at all times.

Mortar A stone bowl that the Romans used for grinding spices.

Mount Olympus The mountain in Greece where the gods were thought to live.

Mulsum A Roman drink made from wine and sweetened with honey.

Mummification A process of drying and embalming by which a dead body is preserved.

Night meal The meal eaten by the Vikings after all the daily work was done, and when it began to grow dark.

Nilometer A measure used to check the water level of the Nile.

Nomarch The official in charge of the running of the region or 'nome'.

Northmen Most of the people the Vikings attacked or traded with knew them as 'Northmen'. 'Viking' was a term they used to describe themselves.

Oracle A holy place in Ancient Greece where the gods could be asked questions with the help of a priest or priestess.

Ostraka A pottery fragment on which Greek citizens wrote the names of the politicians they wished to banish from the city.

Papyrus Ancient Egyptian paper made out of flattened reed stems.

Peplos A long tunic worn in Ancient Greece by women only.

Peristyle The garden of a Roman house with a covered walkway around its edges.

Pharaoh The ruler of ancient Egypt.

Philosopher A person who studies the world about them. In Greece, all great thinkers were known as philosophers.

Polis In Ancient Greece, a state consisting of a city and the surrounding countryside.

Prow The front end of a ship.

Pyramid Tomb with four triangular sides built for the early Egyptian pharaohs.

Republic A state ruled by elected officials instead of a king or emperor.

Rosetta Stone A carved stone which was a major clue to deciphering hieroglyphs. It was found by a French officer in 1799.

Rune A letter of the Viking alphabet. Runes are made up of straight lines as they were intended to be carved on wood or stone.

Sacrifice An offering made to a god to bring good fortune or ask the god not to be angry.

Saga A storytelling adventure of gods or heroes. Although sagas were usually passed on by the Vikings by word of mouth, some were written down.

Scandinavia The group of countries which include Denmark, Norway, Sweden and Iceland.

Senate The official Roman governing council, made up of the heads of the most important families. It gave advice to the consuls and, later, to the emperor.

Senet A game played by the Egyptians with a board and counters.

Slave A worker who was owned by a citizen. In Ancient Greece, slaves had few rights, but they could buy their freedom if they saved enough money.

Soothsayer A person in Ancient Greece, who could predict the future and tell fortunes.

Strigil A curved blade, usually of metal, used in Ancient Greece for scraping oil and dirt from the skin. The Greeks used this method to clean the body, rather than using soap and water.

Sweetmeats A small, sweet snack, popular in Greece, and often made from preserved fruit or nuts.

Symposium A drinking party, held in Ancient Greece, where discussions were held and entertainments may have taken place.

Tablinum A reception room and office, and the most important room in a Roman house.

Valhalla The hall in Asgard where Viking warriors hoped to go when they died. Here they could fight all day and feast all night.

Varangarian Guard A section of the Byzantine army made up of Vikings. The Varangarian Guard was the emperor's bodyguard.

Vizier Chief adviser to the pharaoh. At times there were two of them.

Index